Cooking with Cafe Pasqual's

Cooking with Cafe Pasqual's

RECIPES FROM SANTA FE'S RENOWNED CORNER CAFE

Katharine Kagel

PHOTOGRAPHS BY **KITTY LEAKEN**

TEN SPEED PRESS
Berkeley

Library of Congress Cataloging-in-Publication Data

Kagel, Katharine.
 Cooking with Cafe Pasqual's : recipes from Santa Fe's
renowned corner cafe / Kahtarine Kagel ; photographs
by Kitty Leaken.
    p. cm.
    Includes index.
    1. Cookery, American—Southwestern style. 2.
Cookery, Mexican. 3. Cafe Pasqual's (Santa Fe, N.M.)
I. Cafe Pasqual's (Santa Fe, N.M.) II. Title.
    TX715.2.S69K354 2006
    641.59789—dc22

2005032814

ISBN-13: 978-1-58008-649-3
Printed in Singapore
Designed by Robert Brady and Joseph Shuldiner
12 11 10 9 8
First Edition

Answers

If I envy anyone it must be
My grandmother in a long ago
Green summer, who hurried
Between kitchen and orchard on small
Uneducated feet, and took easily
All shining fruits into her eager hands.

That summer I hurried too, wakened
To books and music and circling philosophies.
I sat in the kitchen sorting through volumes of answers
That could not solve the mystery of the trees.

My grandmother stood among her kettles and ladles.
Smiling, in faulty grammar,
She praised my fortune and urged my lofty career.
So to please her I studied—but I will remember always
How she poured confusion out, how she cooled and labeled
All the wild sauces of the brimming year.

–Mary Oliver

Contents

DINNER

DESSERT

Acknowledgments

IT HAS BEEN A DOZEN YEARS since the publication of our first book, *Cafe Pasqual's Cookbook: Spirited Recipes from Santa Fe*. In reviewing these intervening years, I'm struck at how the world has changed, but the Cafe has basically re-mained the same: our talented key staffers have largely stayed on, as have our regular customers, loyal and true, and many vendors, winemakers, and ranchers, many of whom have become good friends.

Many of the core kitchen crew is still stalwartly ensconced. From the morning crew there is "Can-do," indispensable, dependable, and unflappable Rudy Gabaldon, our master head breakfast chef and ordering captain, as well as ever-cheerful, creative, and fun-loving breakfast/lunch cook Ramon Polanco. Lunch chef Gabriel Ruiz remains our valiant utility infield and MVP for his skillful versatility. He gracefully swings knife or spatula in the a.m. or p.m., pinch-hitting for the baker, line cook, or prep cook. Those magnificent words he says at every turn in the road, "no problema," continue to be music to my ears. Our longtime day crew of Santos Leon, Carlos Pereira, Jesus Pereira, Jesus Rivera, Antonio Caballero, and Emilio Galdamez are major stars in the Pasqual's firmament.

In the evenings, there is skillful Presciliano Ruiz, whose flavor judgment I depend upon. He is the father of all kitchen high jinks, as well as the bringer of delicious and stylish Mexican dishes. Fabulous, hardworking Fritz Fuchs easily cooks on the line, sautés, and grills, working all these stations with great attention to detail. Ricardo Justo prepares our sauces, mole, chiles, salsas, rellenos, and tamales. Consistency is always his uppermost value. Nestor Antonio also can easily switch-hit from a.m. to p.m. crew, bringing his standards of excellence with him wherever he goes. Pablo Rivera, Daniel Rivera, and Balmore Melgar are all known for their brilliant cooking.

Dining manager Brad Brown, *gracias a dios*, still plies the dining room. With his charm, quick smile, and rapier wit, he dazzles us by remembering an astounding roster of the names of our patrons, as well as their likes and dislikes. He easily glides across to work in the gallery and office, effi-

ciently executing a thousand tasks at once. His knowledge of the intricacies of the business and human behavior are deep and invaluable and merit kudos and a thousand thanks.

General manager, David Coulson, aka Mr. Numbers, began working here as a line cook, then moved on to host, waiter, and manager. As general manager, he is our cosmicnaut, a veteran of twenty-one years as of this writing. He continues his heroic dedication to the physical plant, and with his techno-computer wizardry he faithfully keeps track of the numbing numbers. His original, incredibly produced annual movies are legendary and eagerly awaited each year. He also manages to make us all laugh and puzzle with him over the

ambient paradigm and the existential exigencies that are profound when they're not profane. I am grateful that he has been willing to continue to build the Cafe even in the face of tumult, tough times, and meltdowns. His gentle, patient, and generous spirit is unbounded, and I bow.

Robert Brady birthed our gallery, grew it for its first seven years, and showed us the ropes—to him we are so grateful and we salute him. How wonderful and rewarding it has been to work together again, this time on the splendid design of this book, with both Robert and designer Joseph Shuldiner.

For a dozen years, floor manager Bill West has been greeting newcomers and locals alike with his stentorian voice, giving each one stellar dining service. Our Irish lass, Noreen O'Brien, energetically manages the dining room with her twinkling eyes, bright smile, and unending good spirits, also lending a careful expert hand in the gallery and office. Sunshine Lawley greeted the evening's patrons and managed the dining room with elegant aplomb. Tara Esperanza is also a veteran of our evenings. She now adds her sparkle to the evening dining management and is the wine buyer for the ever-changing all-organic wine list. I am deeply grateful to all these and dozens more wondrous, talented, and dedicated staff members, past and present.

Behind the scenes is Lyra Grant, our indefatigable bookkeeper, who keeps rolling out the numbers with good cheer, and Bill Takala, CPA, who continues to tie those buttons and bows with alacrity. There would be no Pasqual's save for Vance Holmes, who, from his working start at age eighteen, is still, at forty-four, plumbing the intricate world of Cafe's heating/ cooling/refrigeration and "pipeage," sometimes at the oddest of hours and for many hours.

My dear friend, Mark Matthiessen, the "ubernitpick" and

playful wordsmith who skillfully edited the first draft of this book, has my eternal gratitude. He made the task a delight, and I shall savor the experience. Nymphe Kefal patiently scribed our elusive never-before-written recipes with patient earnestness. John Vollertsen cooked up a storm for a summer, kicking off the testing and recipe gathering with his laughter and effervescence. To the loyal team of guinea pigs who are ever-true-blue friends to taste and taste and taste— Mark Schilkey, Mia de Sousa, Jan Brooks, Lane Coulter, Malin Wilson, and Greg Powell—*mil gracias*. *Mil gracias* also to Theo Raven, the Cafe's fairy godmother, for her friendship and patronage, and for continuing to point the way. To Kitty Leaken, dear friend, artist, photographer, globe-trotter, and persistent pursuer of inquiry: my deepest thanks for these gorgeous pictures that describe our world so exquisitely.

The knot-tying badge goes to my literary agent, Robert Stricker, for whose support and dedication I am so thankful. A deep bow also to Phil Wood, beacon of Ten Speed Press, and to gracious Jo Ann Deck. A very special thanks to Ten Speed editor Annie Nelson.

To our patrons, whom we have been so privileged to serve over these many years: your friendship, interest, support, loyalty, and good will have buoyed and energized us, and we thank you from the bottom of our hearts.

LEFT: Day chef Gabriel Ruiz **ABOVE:** Dinner chef Presciliano Ruiz

Introduction

WE STARTED CAFE PASQUAL'S twenty-six years ago with a simple idea: serve wonderful, fresh food with friendly service in a festive atmosphere. Over the years, we have become more and more concerned about the quality of the food supply in the United States. There is a need to heed how our food is being raised and handled. We continue our commitment to obtaining organically raised greens, eggs, coffee, dairy, and flour, and naturally raised beef, pork, and chicken.

A reviewer from the *Washington Post* recently described Cafe Pasqual's as being housed in a "festive shoebox," and he is right. Our 650 square feet of dining space has never gotten any bigger, despite pleas from some of our patrons to expand. Cyberspace did expand our boundaries over the past few years, enabling us to send out our specialties: dried chiles, organic coffee blend, granola, five-grain cereal, cookies galore, and, of course, our classic Mexican calendars and art T-shirts, as well as aprons and posters.

We grew another way as well in the years since our first book was published in 1993. We have opened two art galleries upstairs next to the Cafe, where we feature the work of Felipe Ortega, who makes gorgeous handmade utilitarian cooking pots from micaceous clay, in the tradition of the Jicarilla Apache.

We also represent Leovigildo Martinez of Oaxaca, Mexico, who painted the five-panel mural in the Cafe's dining room, *La Luna Se Fe a Una Fiesta*. His ceramics, etchings, lithographs, pen and ink drawings, illustrated children's books, watercolors, and oil paintings are all on view in our galleries.

This compilation of recipes represents gleanings from the past dozen years of the Cafe's offerings. More and more, I have come to realize that my role as a food professional is to be an impresaria, that is, to identify the talent in our staff, or in a recipe, and to bring it into play on our list of offerings. You will see many names in this collection of recipes, for there are many creative artists in our ongoing production. Each brings such special knowledge. For instance, chef Christian Geideman can cook in any cuisine, and you will see recipes of his from India and Thailand. I have always said that what excites me about choosing and presenting Asian dishes is the shared ingredients common to this cuisine and the emphatic flavors of Mexico and El Salvador. I call these shared ingredients of the tropics—lime, mango, coconut, cilantro, ginger, garlic, and chiles—"equatorial cuisine."

It is my sincerest hope that you will enjoy cooking from this collection and seeing the images by Kitty Leaken of our world at Cafe Pasqual's, and that we will be able to give you and yours true nourishment and joy. Our motto remains, *Panza llena, corazon contento!* Full stomach, contented heart!

Pasqual's Pantry

This list of ingredients that are used in the recipes are, for the most part, canned, dried, or bottled and can be readily kept in the pantry or refrigerator. Only a few need to be frozen.

Mexican Ingredients
 Anchos
 Chile de arbol, dried
 Chile flakes (pequín), dried
 Chile powder, medium hot (molido), dried
 Chipotle en adobo (smoked jalapeño in vinegar), canned
 Green chiles, dehydrated
 Guajillo, dried
 Red chiles

**Southeast Asian, Indian,
Middle Eastern, and African Ingredients**
 Asafetida
 Banana leaves, frozen
 Berbere spice, dried
 Black mustard seeds, dried
 Chile sambal, bottled
 Coconut milk, canned
 Coriander seeds, dried
 Cumin, ground
 Curry leaf, dried
 Galangal, fresh (frozen is okay if no reliable fresh source is available)
 Green curry paste, jarred
 Kaffir lime leaves, dried
 Kosher salt
 Lemongrass, fresh (frozen is okay if no reliable fresh source is available)
 Mexican oregano, dried
 Pomegranate molasses, bottled
 Sea salt
 Shrimp paste, jarred, or Thai dried shrimp
 Thai fish sauce, bottled
 Thai jasmine rice
 Thai sticky rice
 White corn flour

Breakfast

Chiles Rellenos y Huevos con Salsa Tomate y Jalapeño

WHEN I WAS A KID, *we would often go downtown and knock around Telegraph Avenue in Berkeley. It's the main shopping street adjacent to the University of California campus. We would either attend a varsity basketball game, or go to the foreign cinema house, or just go and look through the records at the record store, taking them into private listening rooms for a reviewing session. The campus neighborhood teemed with students from all over the world, and the restaurants reflected this marvelous demographic (and still do). We invariably started our evening off at Don Paquin's, our favorite corner Mexican restaurant, where we always indulged in chiles rellenos. At the Cafe, we've figured out a way to serve these morning, noon, and night. Here's the morning version.*

Makes 6 chiles rellenos

ROASTED TOMATO-JALAPEÑO SALSA

3	ripe tomatoes
¼	white onion
1	jalapeño chile
1	clove garlic
1	teaspoon freshly squeezed lime juice
1	tablespoon chopped cilantro leaves
1¾	teaspoons kosher salt

CHILES RELLENOS

6	fresh whole Anaheim chiles
3	cups vegetable oil, plus more for brushing
½	white onion, diced
1½	cups grated Monterey Jack cheese
5	large organic eggs, separated
⅓	cup all-purpose flour
	Pinch of salt
6	large organic eggs, for poaching

TO MAKE THE SALSA, preheat the oven to 400°F. Line a baking sheet with aluminum foil, and on it place the tomatoes, onion, chile, and garlic. Roast in the oven for 25 minutes, turning the ingredients once with tongs. As an alternative, you can roast the vegetables on top of a gas-fueled stove, using a wire-mesh rack placed over a high flame, or on a prepared grill. Roast for 10 minutes, again turning once with tongs. When cool enough to handle, core the tomatoes and stem the jalapeño. (Do not peel the jalapeño.) Put the tomatoes, onion, chile, garlic, lime juice, cilantro, and salt into the container of a blender and whirl for 3 seconds, until incorporated. Do not blend longer because the texture will be lost and the salsa will be too runny.

TO MAKE THE CHILES RELLENOS, preheat the broiler and line a baking sheet with foil. Rinse and dry the chiles. Brush the chiles lightly with vegetable oil, covering the whole surface. Place the chiles on the baking pan and broil for 10 to 15 minutes on each side, until the chiles are blackened and blistered all over. You could also place the chiles directly on the burner, or on a mesh screen over the stove burner, until blackened and blistered. Use tongs to shift, turn, and transfer the chiles so that the juices do not escape. Transfer the chiles to a plastic bag or a cotton cloth dish towel. Seal or wrap the chiles and let them "sweat" for 10 minutes, then stem

OVERLEAF: Dining room manager Brad Brown and office and gallery manager Andy Feinstein

them. Peel by scraping the scorched flesh with a knife, or rub with a nubby terry-cloth towel. Do not rinse the chiles, because the caramelized flavors will be washed away. From the stem end of the chile, gently open the chiles partially and seed carefully with a teaspoon. (Try not to open the sides of the chiles all the way.) Lay out the chiles on paper towels to absorb excess moisture.

PREHEAT THE OVEN to 200°F. Mix the onion and cheese in a small bowl. Squeeze the mixture into 6 equal-sized finger-shaped portions. Stuff each chile with 1 portion.

HEAT THE 3 CUPS OIL in a large deep-sided pan until the oil reaches 350°F. Whip the egg whites in the bowl of an electric mixer until stiff and dry. In a small bowl use a wire whisk to combine the yolks, flour, and salt. Fold gently into the egg whites with a rubber spatula until incorporated.

DIP THE CHILES into the yolk-and-white batter with tongs, holding the dipped chile over the batter bowl to let the excess batter drip. Gently place the battered chiles in the hot oil and cook until browned, turning them once. Place the cooked chiles on a baking sheet covered with a paper towel and keep them warm in the preheated oven. Do not cover the chiles because they will become soggy. Repeat until all the chiles are cooked.

POACH THE EGGS (page 6). When the eggs are done, remove the chiles from the oven. Serve on warmed plates with a poached egg on top. Dab the top of each egg with a kitchen or paper towel to remove the water and ladle some of the salsa over each. (The salsa should either be served at room temperature or warmed.)

Chorizo

THIS ZINGY MEXICAN-STYLE *pork sausage is easy to make and really wakes up dishes with its fabulous flavor. It can be added to scrambled eggs or tofu, quesadillas, dips, soups, pizza, or wherever your culinary journey takes you.*

Makes 2 pounds

2   pounds pork butt, cut into 2-inch cubes
2   tablespoons red wine vinegar
1   teaspoon minced garlic
1   teaspoon stemmed and crumbled chile de arbol
1/2 teaspoon ground cinnamon
2   tablespoons medium-hot red chile powder
2   tablespoons paprika
1   teaspoon dried oregano
2   teaspoons kosher salt
1   teaspoon freshly ground black pepper

PUT ALL THE INGREDIENTS into the bowl of a food processor that is fitted with a steel blade. Pulse the machine until the mixture is well processed. Sauté a tablespoon of the chorizo in a small sauté pan until browned, then test for flavor. Adjust the seasonings in the uncooked portion. Store unused chorizo in serving-size portions in sealed plastic freezer bags for up to 2 months.

Cornmeal Green Chile Waffles with Poached Eggs and Chorizo Gravy

SUNDAY BRUNCH AT THE CAFE *has always featured a special offering, chosen and developed by chef Rudy Galbaldon. This hearty waffle has won rave reviews from our brunch crowd for two decades. As with all successful plans of attack, thoughtful preparation is everything. We make the waffle batter a day ahead of time, and the gravy may be made a day ahead as well; that way, all that's left to do is heat up the waffle iron, pour in the batter, reheat the gravy, and poach the eggs. Buy the freshest organic eggs you can find; the fresher the egg, the higher the yolk will sit on the whites, because the membranes have not broken down. This makes for "poachies" that stay together.* Buen provecho!

Serves 4

CHORIZO GRAVY

6 tablespoons (¾ stick) unsalted butter

2 tablespoons all-purpose flour

2 cups whole milk

½ cup diced white onion

1 cup Mexican-style chorizo (page 5), loose (if using ready-made, remove the casing)

1 teaspoon paprika, plus more for garnish

½ cup ⅛-inch-thick green onion slices, green and white parts, plus 2 tablespoons, for garnish

Pinch of salt

CORNMEAL GREEN CHILE WAFFLES

4 large organic eggs

1½ cups whole milk

¾ cup (1½ sticks) unsalted butter, melted

2¾ teaspoons vanilla extract

1½ cups yellow cornmeal

1½ cups all-purpose flour

1 tablespoon plus 1½ teaspoons baking powder

¾ teaspoon kosher salt

1 tablespoon granulated sugar

4 Anaheim chiles, fresh, fire-roasted, stemmed, peeled, seeded, and diced (see page 2), or ½ ounce dried green chile, hydrated, peeled, and diced

Vegetable oil, liquid, or spray

1 cup pure maple syrup, warmed (optional, in place of chorizo gravy)

POACHED EGGS

2 tablespoons white vinegar

8 eggs

TO MAKE THE GRAVY, prepare a roux by placing 2 tablespoons of the butter into a saucepan over medium heat. When the butter is sizzling, add the flour and whisk with a wire balloon whisk. Continue whisking until the roux becomes golden in color and a bit "dry" in appearance. Add all the milk. Turn up the heat to medium-high and whisk for 3 to 5 minutes, until the gravy thickens. Remove from the heat and set aside.

IN A 10-INCH SAUTÉ PAN over medium heat, add the remaining 4 tablespoons butter and the onion. Sauté the onion until it is translucent, about 4 minutes, stirring

large mixing bowl, combine the cornmeal, flour, baking powder, salt, and sugar. Mix until blended. Pour the dry ingredients into the wet ingredients and use a wooden spoon to mix thoroughly. Add in the chiles and stir.

HEAT A WAFFLE IRON. When it is hot and the "ready" display light is lit, spray the interior with vegetable oil, or use a paper towel with a tablespoon of oil on it to wipe down the iron's interior so that the waffles will not stick. Ladle a generous ½ cup of the batter into the waffle iron and cook until golden brown. Hold all the finished waffles in the preheated oven in a pan or on a plate, uncovered, until all the batter has been used. Preheat 4 plates.

TO POACH THE EGGS, fill a 12-inch straight-sided nonreactive sauté pan with water until three-fourths filled, and then add the vinegar. The addition of vinegar helps ensure that the eggs will remain egg-shaped and that the whites will not stream about the pan. Place the skillet over high heat. Crack an egg one at a time into a shallow bowl and when the water is simmering, slip the egg into the water. Repeat, cooking the eggs in 2 batches of 4 eggs each. Cook the eggs for 4 to 5 minutes, until the whites are firm but the yolks are still soft inside.

WHILE THE EGGS ARE COOKING, put 2 waffles on each of 4 preheated plates. Remove and drain the eggs with a slotted spoon and put one on each of the waffles. Gently dab the tops of the eggs with a paper towel or kitchen towel to blot the water so that the gravy will adhere. Serve with warmed chorizo gravy and garnish with the reserved chorizo, the green onion slices, and a pinch of paprika. (If you prefer, you may substitute maple syrup for the gravy.)

occasionally. Add the chorizo and cook for 10 minutes, stirring occasionally, until the chorizo browns. Stir in 1 teaspoon paprika and ½ cup green onions and cook for 4 more minutes. Transfer ½ cup of the chorizo mixture to a bowl, and reserve for garnish. Add the roux to the rest of the chorizo and whisk until blended. Add salt to taste.

TO MAKE THE WAFFLES, preheat the oven to 200°F. Break the eggs into a large bowl and add the milk, melted butter, and vanilla. Whisk until incorporated. In another

Five-Grain Cereal

DAVID COULSON *has been our general manager for the last fifteen of his twenty-one years at the Cafe. He began his tenure as a line cook, and developed this recipe for one of our regular customers who asked him to put the grain teff on our menu, due to an intolerance to wheat and oats. Teff is the world's smallest grain ($\frac{1}{32}$ inch). There is no gluten in teff and it also has a high percentage of bran and germ, making it rich in protein, minerals, and fiber. Not only is this cereal combination delicious, but it also has that stick-to-your-ribs quality that will stave off hunger for the better part of a day.*

Makes 12 servings

CEREAL MIXTURE
- 1 cup barley flakes
- 1 cup rye flakes
- $\frac{1}{2}$ cup whole millet
- $\frac{1}{4}$ cup amaranth
- $\frac{1}{4}$ cup teff

Mix all the ingredients in a bowl. Store in an airtight container.

Makes 4 servings

- 4 cups water
- Pinch of kosher salt
- 1 cup cereal mixture (above)
- 4 tablespoons ($\frac{1}{2}$ stick) butter
- $\frac{1}{4}$ cup pure maple syrup

BRING THE WATER TO A BOIL in a large saucepan. Add the salt and cereal grains and lower the heat to medium-low; leave the pan uncovered. Stir the mixture frequently until the cereal is creamy and soft in texture, about 40 minutes. Spoon the cereal into 4 bowls and add a tablespoon of butter and a tablespoon of maple syrup to each serving. Serve immediately.

Linda's Golden Granola

FOR NINE GLORIOUS YEARS *at the Cafe we were lucky enough to work with Linda Schulak-Cook, who played significant roles in both the front and the back of the house. Manager, hostess, food purchaser, and baker, she brought her own pizzazz to each job. This is "the granola for all time," a recipe she developed with great care. If you should want this recipe already made up, the Café's kitchen sends out bags of it to our mail-order customers (see page 147).*

Makes 1½ pounds granola (12 cups)

½ cup vegetable oil
½ cup honey
½ cup pure maple syrup
½ cup smooth peanut butter
½ cup apple juice
1½ teaspoons cinnamon
1½ teaspoons ground ginger
¼ teaspoon ground cloves
4 cups rolled oats (not instant)
2 cups bran
½ cup chopped pecans
½ cup pecan halves
1 cup almond halves (with skin)
¼ cup whole cashews
¾ cup shredded coconut, unsweetened

PREHEAT THE OVEN to 300°F. In the container of a blender, put in the oil, honey, syrup, peanut butter, apple juice, cinnamon, ginger, and cloves. Mix well. Remove the mixture to a large mixing bowl and add the oats, bran, both types of pecans, almonds, and cashews. Mix thoroughly.

SPREAD THE COCONUT on a jelly-roll pan and bake in the oven for 20 minutes. Stir once halfway through the cooking time. Let cool and reserve. Use two metal baking pans that measure 19 inches by 12 inches by 1¾ inches high, and line each with a piece of parchment paper. Divide the granola equally between the pans and toast for 1 hour, stirring occasionally, until the granola has an allover golden color. Remove from the oven and add the toasted coconut. When the granola has cooled completely, store it in an airtight container for future use.

Red Chile and Sugar-Cured Bacon

ONCE UPON A TIME *in the late '80s, chef Sally Witham graced our kitchen and brought us this insanely delicious breakfast treat that we served with waffles. We've since offered it on our BLT (bacon, lettuce, and tomato sandwich) and it always garners rave reviews. Don't make this without parchment paper to cover the baking sheets or the bacon will stick like the dickens.*

Serves 4

2	tablespoons mild red chile powder
¾	cup firmly packed brown sugar
12	thick-sliced pieces applewood-smoked bacon (approximately 8 ounces)

PREHEAT THE OVEN to 300°F. Mix the chile powder and sugar in a shallow bowl. Fit a sheet of parchment paper onto a jelly-roll pan. Bury each slice of bacon in the chile and sugar mixture and rub both sides to assure the mixture adheres. Lay the bacon strips on the prepared pan. The bacon strips may be left flat or twisted two or three times by holding each end to make a candied "stick." Bake for 30 minutes without turning. Always transfer candied bacon using tongs; the hot sugar can easily burn your fingers.

Smoked Trout Hash with Poached Eggs and Tomatillo Salsa

THIS IS A VERY POPULAR *dish at the Cafe. It's one of those recipes that engages all parts of the tongue: salty, sweet, and zesty all at once. Smoked trout is widely available in the deli departments of supermarkets, usually located close to the smoked salmon. Fresh tomatillos are easily found in most natural foods groceries, good supermarkets, and in all Latin groceries. Buy the freshest organic eggs you can, because the integrity of the white and yolk will be pronounced and easy to poach. Taste the salsa before use, as you may decide to add another jalapeño or chile de arbol, depending on your preference and your tolerance for things piquant.*

Serves 4

TOMATILLO SALSA

10	large tomatillos, husked and rinsed
1 or 2	jalapeño chiles, stemmed and halved
¼	white onion, coarsely chopped
1	clove garlic
20	sprigs cilantro, including stems
1 or 2	chiles de arbol, stemmed
2	cups tightly packed spinach leaves
1½	teaspoons kosher salt

HASH BROWN POTATO CAKES

4	russet baking potatoes (2 pounds), peeled
1	cup grated Gruyère cheese (4 ounces)
¼	cup finely minced fresh chives
1½	teaspoons kosher salt
1½	teaspoons freshly ground black pepper
5	tablespoons butter
8	large eggs, for poaching
1	pound smoked trout, torn into 3- by 1-inch pieces
	Parsley or cilantro sprigs, for garnish

TO MAKE THE SALSA, put all the ingredients into the container of a blender. Whirl until liquefied. Taste for heat and add more chiles if desired. Transfer to a serving bowl.

TO MAKE THE POTATO CAKES, in a large stockpot, bring enough water to cover the potatoes to a boil. Add the potatoes and cook for 20 minutes at high heat, or until a fork piercing the potato just slips in. (Do not overcook.) Drain the water and let the potatoes cool completely. This may take as long as 3 hours. You may want to cook the potatoes a day in advance and refrigerate them, because they need to be absolutely cool for grating. Grate the potatoes on a hand grater. In a large bowl, mix the potatoes, cheese, chives, salt, and pepper, gently lifting and tossing the ingredients with your hands.

PREHEAT THE OVEN to 200°F. Put 1 tablespoon of the butter into a preheated 7-inch nonstick skillet and allow the butter to cover the pan. When the butter is heated, hand pat one-fourth of the potato mixture into the pan. Sauté the potatoes over medium-high heat, 3 to 4 minutes per side, or until golden. Repeat for the remaining 3 potato pancakes. Keep the potato cakes warm in the oven, until the whole dish is ready for assembly. Preheat 4 plates.

POACH THE EGGS (page 6). While the eggs are cooking, begin to assemble the dish. Place the potato pancakes on the warmed plates. Put the remaining 1 tablespoon of butter in a sauté pan, add the trout and heat through, about 1 minute on each side.

WHEN THE EGGS ARE OPAQUE in appearance, lift them out of the water with a slotted spoon, letting them drain over the pan. Place 2 poached eggs on top of each of the potato pancakes. Gently dab the top of each egg with a kitchen or paper towel to dry the eggs so that the tomatillo salsa will not slide off. Spoon 2 tablespoons of tomatillo salsa over the eggs and scatter the trout around the potato pancake. Serve the remaining salsa in a bowl for those who may want more. Garnish with parsley or cilantro sprigs.

Tamales Dulces

THIS IS A TRADITIONAL *syrup-infused breakfast tamal recipe from El Salvador, contributed by chef Napoleon Lopez. Banana leaf is my favorite wrapping for tamales. The rectangular package with its leaf-strip tie is intriguing, but more than that, the banana leaf has a special aroma that transports one to the tropics. The leaves can be purchased in large packages from the frozen foods section of most Asian or Latin groceries. To thaw, simply put the whole package unopened in a pan of hot water, keeping the water hot until thawed. We use white corn flour grown by the Iroquois Nation (see page 148). It is roasted before it is ground, giving it a particularly toasty flavor that is perfect for breakfast comfort food. These tamales can be frozen for up to 2 months. Do not turn the tamal out of the leaf when serving; instead, unwrap the banana leaf package and enjoy eating right off the leaf. At the Cafe we serve them as a hearty breakfast with half a fresh mango, black beans, and a mug of Mexican hot chocolate alongside.*

Makes 12 tamales

1½ cups pure maple syrup
6 whole star anise
5 whole cloves
1 orange, quartered
½ stick Mexican cinnamon (canela)
4 cups water
1½ cups masa harina or white corn flour
2 tablespoons sultana (golden) raisins
3 tablespoons dry sherry
1 package frozen banana leaves,
    8 by 10 inches long, thawed
¾ cup asadero cheese or
    Monterey Jack cheese, grated
2 bananas, cut in half lengthwise,
    then cut into thirds
¾ cup fresh corn kernels
    (cut from 1 ear of corn)
2 tablespoons piñon nuts (pine nuts), toasted

PUT THE SYRUP, anise, cloves, orange quarters, and cinnamon stick into a heavy-bottomed saucepan over medium-high heat. Bring to a boil and simmer for 5 minutes. Turn off the heat and allow the spiced syrup to cool.

BRING THE WATER to a boil in a large saucepan. Slowly pour in the masa harina and stir with a wire whisk for 8 to 10 minutes, or until the masa is thickened. Remove from the heat. Strain the syrup and spice mixture into a bowl and discard the spice mix. Add the flavored syrup to the masa and mix with a wooden spoon.

PUT THE RAISINS in a small bowl and add the sherry. Allow them to soak for about 20 minutes. Drain the raisins.

FOR THE TIES, make 12 (8-inch-long by ¼-inch-wide) strips from one of the banana leaves. (Rip the leaves in the natural direction of the fibers.) Use a rubber spatula to spread ½ cup of the masa onto the middle of each banana leaf, making a 3- by 5-inch rectangle. Make a small depression in the middle of each masa rectangle

and into that put 1 tablespoon of the cheese, one of the banana pieces, 1 tablespoon of corn, ½ teaspoon of piñon nuts, and ½ teaspoon of raisins. Repeat to make the remaining tamales.

TO WRAP, take the long side of the rectangle to just past the center, then bring the opposite side up and over the first. Fold up each end to form a package. Use the leaf strips to wrap the tamales from end to end. Tie with a double knot.

TO STEAM THE TAMALES, put them in a multitiered steamer pot over boiling water, and cook for 1½ hours. (Be sure to check the water level of the steamer occasionally and refill the water as needed.) Serve hot. To reheat the tamales, it is best to re-steam them for 15 to 20 minutes, but if time is of the essence you may microwave them for about 2 minutes.

Whole-Wheat Pancakes

RUDY GABALDON *has been our acclaimed and cherished breakfast chef for twenty-one years as of this writing. He has been making these perfected stacks for all that time, listed on our menu as "Pasqual's Favorite." When making "the Favorite," add a couple of eggs, any style, on top of the cakes. You can also lay alongside each stack two sausage links or two strips of bacon, as we do. Serve the cakes with butter and pure maple syrup.*

Makes 12 pancakes

3	large organic eggs
1⅓	cups milk
½	cup vegetable oil
⅓	cup honey
2	cups plus 2 teaspoons whole-wheat flour
1	tablespoon plus 1 teaspoon baking powder
1	teaspoon kosher salt
½	cup (1 stick) unsalted butter, melted, plus ½ cup (1 stick) unsalted butter
	Pure maple syrup, warmed

PREHEAT THE OVEN to 200°F. Break the eggs into a large mixing bowl. Mix briskly with a wire balloon whisk until the yolk and white are incorporated. Add the milk, vegetable oil, and honey. Whisk until the mixture is smooth and the honey has dissolved.

IN A SEPARATE BOWL, sift together the whole-wheat flour, baking powder, and salt. Add in batches to the egg mixture and whisk until smooth.

HEAT A 7-INCH NONSTICK sauté pan over medium heat and brush with some of the melted butter. Ladle ⅓ cup of the batter into the pan and tilt the pan to cover the bottom evenly with batter. Allow each pancake to cook until bubbles appear on the surface. Flip the pancake with a nonmetal spatula and cook the second side another 3 minutes, or until browned. (It is important to use a nonmetal spatula when using a nonstick pan, otherwise you'll scratch the pan's surface.) If you are adept, you may flip the pancake without a hand tool, using the pan itself, flapjack style.

AS EACH PANCAKE is finished cooking, transfer it to an ovenproof plate in the oven. Do not cover the pancakes, because the resulting condensation will make them soggy. If you have a griddle, use that instead of a pan, or use two pans at once in order to shorten the cooking time. Repeat this process, brushing the pan with melted butter for each cake, until you have 12 pancakes, kept warm in the oven. Serve with the stick of butter and warmed maple syrup alongside.

Soup

Andalusian White Gazpacho

THIS WHITE GAZPACHO *can surprise the uninitiated who think that a gazpacho must have tomatoes to qualify for the title. The word gazpacho means "soaked bread," which serves as the thickener for this version. Andalusia is located in the south of Spain, which is blazing hot in the summer. This recipe, when well chilled, provides the perfect antidote.*

Serves 6

7 cucumbers, peeled, seeded,
   and coarsely chopped
3 or 4 cloves garlic
2 ounces blanched almonds, plus additional
   toasted almonds, for garnish
1 cup bread pieces, crusts removed
3 tablespoons manzanilla sherry
   or dry white wine
1 tablespoon extra virgin olive oil
1 cup ice cubes
¼ pound green seedless grapes, washed,
   plus ¼ pound, cut in half, for garnish
1 teaspoon salt
   Edible flowers, for garnish (optional)

PLACE ALL THE INGREDIENTS, except the garnishes, into the container of a blender and puree until smooth. Taste and adjust for garlic or salt additions. Chill until cold and serve garnished with toasted almonds, cut seedless grapes, and edible flowers.

Carrot, Marsala, and Ginger Soup

THIS SPICY SOUP *is an oldie but goodie from the Cafe's repertoire. Look for the best quality imported dry Marsala from Sicily, which has a smoky-nutty aroma and is rich with wood flavors. This soup may be served chilled or hot.*

Serves 6

4	tablespoons (½ stick) unsalted butter
2	pounds carrots, peeled and diced
2	yellow onions, diced
4	cups water
¼	teaspoon cayenne pepper
¼	teaspoon ground ginger
¼	teaspoon ground white pepper
	Zest and juice of 1 orange
¼	cup plus 1 tablespoon imported dry Marsala wine
1	cup half-and-half
½	teaspoon kosher salt
	Paprika, for garnish

PUT THE BUTTER into a large saucepan over medium-high heat, and when it has melted, add the carrots and onion. Sauté until the onion is translucent. Add the water, cayenne, ginger, and pepper. Simmer a few more minutes until the carrots are fork-tender. Add the orange zest, orange juice, Marsala, and half-and-half. Puree in batches in a food processor or the container of a blender until smooth and velvety. Add the salt and adjust to taste, and add more of the ground spices as your palate dictates. Heat when ready to serve, but do not boil. Sprinkle with paprika for garnish.

RIGHT: Carlos Pereira, Antonio Nestor, and Balmore Melgar all contribute hugely to the Cafe's cuisine

Chicken Stock

THIS RICH AND DELICIOUS *stock is the gold standard. Regard this recipe as more of an outline, something to play and have fun with. Feel free to add your favorite flavors: use cilantro instead of parsley, for instance, or yellow or white onions instead of green. Double up the chile for extra sensation, or add slices of fresh ginger or other favorite aromatics. Please remember that any chicken stock is fragile and should be used within 48 hours. When reheating stock within that time frame, always boil it for 10 minutes to kill any bacteria that may be present. Stock may be frozen for up to 2 months.*

Makes 10 cups

4 quarts water

1 (4-pound) chicken, or 4 pounds chicken backs and wings, or other parts in combination (if meat yield is not important)

6 green onions, green and white parts, cut into fourths

1 bunch flat-leaf parsley, including stems

8 ounces carrots, cut into chunks

3 stalks celery, cut into fourths

8 whole cloves

1 chile de arbol, broken in half

1½ teaspoons kosher salt

1 teaspoon freshly ground black pepper

PUT THE WATER into an 8-quart stockpot over high heat, and add the chicken, green onions, parsley, carrots, celery, cloves, and chile. Bring the stock to a rolling boil. Skim off any foam that forms on the surface of the broth and discard. Turn down the heat to maintain a bare simmer and let simmer for 2½ hours uncovered. Add the salt and pepper.

LINE A STRAINER with cheesecloth and set over a large container. Pour the stock through the cheesecloth.

REMOVE THE MEATIER cuts of the chicken, and when cool, pick the meat from the bones. Discard the skin and shred the meat and save for future use by freezing, or use within 48 hours. Store the stock overnight in the refrigerator, then remove the fat from the top. (Either save the fat for another use or discard it.) Use the stock immediately or freeze it.

Beet and Chipotle Soup

YOU CAN'T BEAT A BEET *for sheer entertainment value. It intrigues us with its rich burgundy color and aroma of wet gardens. It bleeds all its color if the stem is shorn, and it is dull on the outside but dazzling on the inside. The flavor, while so sweet, is capable of carrying dark mysterious tastes to our tongues. Save the beet leaves (if attached) for another purpose, as they make a great steamed green or stir-fry ingredient. This recipe adds chiles en adobo, which are smoked jalapeños in a vinegary sauce. They come in a can; when opened and transferred to a glass container, they may be kept for months in the refrigerator. Chiles en adobo can be used to spice up all manner of food: stews, sauces, mayonnaise, eggs, dips, or wherever the spice of life is needed. Play with it, but use it sparingly because it is hot hot hot.*

Serves 4 to 6

2	pounds whole beets
1½	cups chicken stock (page 27)
1	cup full-bodied red wine
6	cups water
¼	cup (½ stick) unsalted butter
1	white onion, coarsely chopped
1	tablespoon dark brown sugar
2	tablespoons red wine vinegar
½	cup freshly squeezed lemon juice
½	cup sour cream, plus ¼ cup, for garnish
2	chipotle chiles en adobo
	Fresh chives, snipped fine, for garnish

TRIM THE LEAVES from the beets, leaving 1 inch of the stem and the entire root intact. Put the beets, stock, and wine into a large soup pot, and add the water. The liquid should cover the beets by at least 1 inch. Bring to a boil and let simmer, covered, for 45 minutes to 1 hour. Fork-test the beets for tenderness before removing them from the pot. Remove the beets with a slotted spoon, and reserve the cooking liquid in the soup pot. When the beets have cooled enough to handle, peel them and remove the stems and roots. Cut up a ½ cup of ½-inch diced beets for garnish and set aside. Coarsely chop the remaining beets and set aside.

HEAT THE BUTTER in a large saucepan over medium heat, and when it is melted, add the onion and brown sugar. Sauté for 2 minutes, stirring with a wooden spoon, until the sugar is dissolved. Add the onions, coarsely chopped beets, red wine vinegar, lemon juice, ½ cup sour cream, and chiles en adobo to the beet liquid in the soup pot. Whirl everything in the container of a blender until smooth, in batches if need be. The soup can be served hot or cold; if cold, chill it in the refrigerator, covered, for at least 6 hours. Garnish with the reserved beets and 1 tablespoon of sour cream, then garnish with chives.

Citrus Gazpacho

THIS MUCH-REQUESTED *summertime recipe never fails to engender sighs of satisfaction. It was developed by chef Kelly Rogers, who used to manage the Cafe's kitchen. The trick to this recipe is to cut all the diced ingredients into uniform dimensions. I like to serve this soup as a starter in martini or cocktail glasses during the "meet and greet" part of a party. It refreshes and picks up the spirit. It is easy to adjust the heat or sweetness to suit the palates of you and your guests.*

Makes 6 cups

4	large ripe tomatoes
1	clove garlic, minced
1	tablespoon white wine vinegar
2½	cups freshly squeezed orange juice
	Zest and fruit of 1 orange
	Zest of ½ and fruit of 1 pink grapefruit
½	cucumber, peeled, seeded, and diced
½	yellow bell pepper, stemmed, seeded, and diced
¼	medium red onion, diced
1	tablespoon olive oil
1	teaspoon kosher salt
½	teaspoon freshly ground black pepper
	Cayenne pepper

FILL A LARGE SAUCEPAN with enough water to cover the tomatoes. Place over high heat and bring to a full boil. While the water is heating, use the tip of a sharp paring knife to score a small X on the bottom of each tomato, just piercing the skin. Put the tomatoes into the boiling water for 20 seconds. Use tongs to transfer the tomatoes to a large bowl filled with ice and water. (This will stop further cooking.) Allow the tomatoes to cool for a few minutes, remove them from the water, and peel their skins with either a paring knife or your fingers, starting at the scored end. Discard the peel. Core and dice one tomato and reserve it. Slice the other tomatoes in half crosswise, and squeeze out the seeds. Remove the cores. Put the tomatoes into the container of a blender. Place the garlic, vinegar, orange juice, and orange and grapefruit zests into the blender with the tomatoes and whirl. Transfer the puree to a serving pitcher or a serving bowl and add the cucumber, bell pepper, red onion, and olive oil.

TO PREPARE THE FRUIT, use a paring knife on a cutting board to cut off both ends of the grapefruit and orange so that the fruit can securely stand on end for cutting. Starting from the top of the citrus, slice off all the peel and pith, following the contour. All the fruit will now be exposed. Cradle the fruit in the palm of the hand you aren't using for slicing, and use the paring knife to cut loose each fruit segment from the inner side of the membrane. Angle the long side of the blade between the fruit and the membrane and toward the center of each segment, cutting in a V configuration. No membrane should now be attached to the fruit segments. Add the fruit segments to the gazpacho mixture and stir. Add the salt, pepper, and cayenne to taste. Chill well before serving.

Avogolemono with Cucumber and Mint

THIS IS A LIGHT *but very nourishing soup. It was contributed by my friend Nymphe Kefal, a daughter of Greece. She not only gave us this recipe but also shared her keen observations during the gathering of recipes for this book. Orzo is a fun, semolina wheat-based pasta masquerading in the shape of rice. It can be found in most supermarkets in the pasta section.*

Serves 4

4	cups chicken stock (page 27)
2	large organic eggs, beaten
1/2	cup freshly squeezed lemon juice
1	cup plain whole-milk yogurt
1/2	teaspoon ground white pepper
1	cup peeled, seeded, and diced cucumber
1	cup cooked orzo or white rice (follow instructions on the package)
1	tablespoon fresh mint, stemmed and finely minced, plus more for garnish
1/2	teaspoon kosher salt
1	lemon, thinly sliced, for garnish (optional)

BRING THE CHICKEN STOCK to a boil in a large saucepan. Whisk the eggs in a large bowl until well beaten, then slowly add the lemon juice. In a thin stream, slowly add 1 cup of the hot chicken stock to the egg and lemon mixture. Add this mixture very slowly to the remaining stock, and turn down the heat to medium. Do not allow the soup to boil because this will spoil the silky consistency. Cook for 3 minutes so the soup will thicken slightly. Remove from the heat and whisk in the yogurt, white pepper, cucumber, orzo, mint, and salt.

SERVE HOT OR COLD. Garnish with mint sprigs and/or lemon slices.

Napo's Caldo de Pollo y Salsa de Chile Rojo

THIS TUMMY-WARMING SOUP *from chef Napoleon Lopez gives a truly satisfying experience. It includes two very important techniques of south-of-the-border cooking: the charring of the ingredients and their subsequent sautéing in oil, a defining mark of this cuisine. Cooking twice maximizes flavors; shortcuts just don't provide the same results. To char the veggies, place a wire-mesh frame (available from most kitchen shops) over an open flame on high on a gas-fueled stove. A* comal *(Spanish for a flat, flameproof clay or metal surface) may also be employed to roast the vegetables (or you can use your broiler). Spices are frequently toasted in their powder form before adding to a recipe, also maximizing flavor. A pound of peeled and deveined shrimp may be substituted for the chicken. Cook the shrimp until they just turn pink, keeping the rest of the procedure the same.*

Serves 6

STOCK

3 pounds chicken parts: thighs, wings, necks, backs, drumsticks, in combination, rinsed under cold water

2 cloves garlic, slightly crushed

½ large white onion, coarsely chopped

1 carrot, peeled and coarsely chopped

1 celery stalk, cut into thirds

1 chile de arbol

2 bay leaves

4 whole cloves

10 black peppercorns

1 tablespoon salt

8 cups cold water

SOUP

¼ cup olive oil

2 ears corn, shucked

4 tomatoes

1 white onion, quartered

2 cloves garlic

2 fresh whole poblano chiles

6 green onions, white and green parts, cut into fourths

½ cup red chile sauce (page 76)

1 teaspoon kosher salt

½ teaspoon freshly ground black pepper

½ teaspoon ground cumin, toasted in a dry pan over medium heat until fragrant, 2 to 3 minutes

½ cup cilantro leaves, minced, for garnish

TO MAKE THE STOCK, place all the ingredients into a large stockpot and bring to a boil. Reduce the heat to a low simmer and cook uncovered for 1 hour, until the chicken is falling off the bones. Remove the chicken pieces and set aside. Strain the stock through a fine-mesh sieve and reserve. When the chicken has cooled enough to handle, pull the meat from the bones, cover, and refrigerate.

TO MAKE THE SOUP, preheat a charcoal or gas grill. Place 2 tablespoons of the oil into a large bowl. Add the corn, tomatoes, onion, garlic, poblano chiles, and green

onions, and toss to coat in the oil. Grill the vegetables over high heat until all are nicely charred and the poblano and tomato skins are blistered all over. Allow the vegetables to cool, then peel and core the tomatoes and peel and stem the poblano. Cut the corn from the cob with a large, sharp knife.

ROUGHLY CHOP the roasted tomatoes, onion, poblano chiles, and green onions and place them in the bowl of a food processor fitted with a steel blade or the container of a blender with just enough water to move the blades (about ¼ cup), along with the garlic and corn. Pulse to blend slightly, still leaving the vegetables in small chunks.

HEAT THE REMAINING 2 tablespoons of olive oil in a large soup pot and add the vegetables to the pot. Sauté them for 5 minutes over medium heat. Add the stock, chicken, red chile sauce, salt, pepper, and cumin and simmer for 5 more minutes. Add the cilantro garnish just before serving.

Pecan Chipotle Soup

THIS THICK AND DELICIOUS SOUP *hails from Iliana de la Vega, genius chef/owner of El Naranjo restaurant. Her restaurant is my oasis when I travel to Oaxaca, Mexico. Chef de la Vega's cuisine bursts with the bright flavors of the region, and this unique soup is piquant, nourishing, and unforgettable. It gets its luxurious thickness from the pecans and sprightly flavors from the chipotle chiles and garlic.*

Serves 4

2	tablespoons butter
1	teaspoon vegetable oil
1	large clove garlic, pressed
1	slice stale bread, whole wheat or white, torn into 8 pieces, crusts removed and discarded
1¼	cups pecan pieces (¼ pound)
½	pound ripe tomatoes, quartered
2	chipotle chiles en adobo
4	cups whole milk
	Large pinch of kosher salt
½	teaspoon freshly ground black pepper
10	sprigs parsley, finely minced, for garnish

MELT THE BUTTER and oil in a saucepan over medium heat. Add the garlic, bread, and pecans to the saucepan and sauté until golden. In the container of a blender, in batches if need be, place the sautéed mixture, tomatoes, chipotles, and milk. Blend until smooth, and then pour into a saucepan. Bring to a simmer over medium heat and cook for 3 minutes, or until the soup is heated through, stirring frequently. Add the salt and pepper and serve hot in warmed bowls. Garnish with the parsley.

KK's Elixir

THIS IS MY OWN *zingy elixir, a liquid salad that awakens and sustains through the dog days of summer. It's quick and easy whirled up in the blender. I like the pronounced flavors of garlic and red wine vinegar, but you can adjust them to suit your own palate.*

Serves 4

- 2 pounds ripe tomatoes (about 9 tomatoes), cored and cut into quarters
- 1/2 pound peeled, seeded, and coarsely chopped cucumbers
- 1/2 cup coarsely chopped yellow onion
- 2 cloves garlic, pressed
- 1 jalapeño, stemmed, seeded, and cut into quarters
- 1/4 cup red wine vinegar
- 2 tablespoons olive oil
- 3/4 teaspoon kosher salt
- 1 cup croutons, for garnish (page 41)

PLACE ALL THE INGREDIENTS except the croutons into the container of a blender and whirl until smooth. Refrigerate until well chilled and serve in icy-cold bowls or glasses. Garnish with croutons.

San Marzano Tomato Soup with Croutons

THIS IS A FABULOUS RECIPE *from chef Christian Geideman, who has since opened his own restaurant, Kasaboba, in Santa Fe. I am a devoted fan of his work and a haunt at his restaurant. Here is a very simple, rich, and homey soup that will bring a smile to your lips. Look for San Marzano canned tomatoes from Italy; they come in a large can and are packed in their own juice. The domestic label that bears the same name is not at all comparable in flavor to this Italian import.*

Serves 6

7 tablespoons unsalted butter

6 slices French baguette, cut
   into ½-inch by ½-inch cubes

1 tablespoon kosher salt

2 tablespoons minced white onion

1 large can (28 ounces) San Marzano whole
   tomatoes, chopped, juice reserved

1 bay leaf

2 tablespoons sugar

½ cup bread crumbs, grated from
   toasted French baguette

4 cups whole milk

2 tablespoons finely minced flat-leaf parsley,
   or 6 basil leaves, for garnish
   Freshly ground black pepper, for garnish

PREHEAT THE OVEN to 400°F. Melt 4 tablespoons of the butter in a 10-inch frying pan, and stir in the bread cubes. Sauté over medium heat until the bread begins to brown. Sprinkle all with ½ teaspoon of the salt, toss together, and bake on a cookie sheet for 10 minutes or until golden, stirring occasionally. Remove the croutons from the oven and set aside.

MELT THE REMAINING 3 tablespoons of butter in a 4-quart nonreactive pot over medium heat. Add the onions and sauté for 3 minutes, or until they are translucent. Add the tomatoes and their juice, bay leaf, and sugar and sauté for 10 minutes. Stir in the bread crumbs.

REMOVE FROM THE HEAT and stir in the milk. (The mixture will curdle slightly.) Remove the bay leaf. Puree in batches in the container of a blender until the soup is smooth, and then return the soup to a simmer over medium heat. Season with the remaining 2½ teaspoons of salt and adjust. If using basil leaves for garnish, chiffonade them by stacking the leaves together and rolling them up tightly. Slice the rolled leaves into very small rounds to make narrow strips. Unfurl the strips for garnish. Serve immediately with garnishes of croutons, minced parsley or basil, and a grind of black pepper.

Salad

Caesar Salad with Carne Asada

THIS FAMOUS SALAD, *combined with grilled piquant beef strips (called carne asada in Spanish), makes for an entire spectacular meal. It is crisp and juicy, the perfect marriage. There are many parts to this recipe, but once organized, timed properly, and assembled, it is truly worth the journey. Invest in a really good stainless steel garlic press—it's a great way to access garlic's natural juices.*

Serves 4

CROUTONS

¾ cup (1½ sticks) unsalted butter, melted

2 cloves garlic, pressed

2 tablespoons paprika or other favorite mild red chile powder

2 cups cubed stale French bread, crusts removed

3 tablespoons finely minced flat-leafed parsley

CAESAR DRESSING

½ cup plus 1 tablespoon sherry vinegar

1 tablespoon Dijon mustard

2 ounces (1 can) anchovy fillets, drained

2 tablespoons freshly squeezed lemon juice

¼ cup grated Parmegiano-Reggiano cheese

¼ cup extra virgin olive oil

2 large organic eggs, at room temperature

SALAD

2 large heads romaine lettuce, outer leaves discarded, or 4 hearts of romaine

1½ pounds grilled carne asada, cut into 2-inch strips (page 63)

1 cup thinly shaved Parmegiano-Reggiano cheese

TO MAKE THE CROUTONS, preheat the oven to 300°F. In a small bowl, mix the butter, garlic, and paprika together. Put the bread cubes into a large bowl, pour on the butter mixture, and stir to coat evenly. Add the parsley. Spread the croutons onto a baking sheet and place in the preheated oven, stirring frequently for 20 minutes, or until browned. Let the croutons cool.

TO MAKE THE DRESSING, place the vinegar, mustard, anchovies, lemon juice, and cheese into the container of a blender and puree until smooth. While the motor is still running, slowly drizzle the olive oil into the blender. Remove to a glass container, cover, and refrigerate. When ready to dress the salad, coddle the eggs by lowering them into a saucepan with enough boiling water to cover. Turn off the heat, cover the pan, and let sit for 1 minute. Remove the eggs from the water and crack in half. Add the coddled whites and yolks to the dressing mixture, and whisk vigorously with a wire balloon whisk.

TO MAKE THE SALAD, wash and spin dry the lettuce leaves, then lay them out on dry paper towels. Roll them up in the paper and put them into the refrigerator's crisper bin. When well chilled, place the lettuce leaves in a bowl, add the dressing, and toss. Divide the lettuce among 4 serving plates. Place equal portions of the carne asada strips over the leaves and scatter the cheese shavings and croutons on top. Serve immediately.

Dana's Fennel, Roasted Yellow Pepper, and Rosemary Salad

IT SEEMS LIKE A GAZILLION *years ago (at least twenty) that we had a very talented cook at the Cafe, unfortunately remembered now only as Dana from Connecticut. This is her simple but perfect Mediterranean salad.*

Serves 4

3	large yellow bell peppers
1	large fennel bulb
2	tablespoons freshly squeezed orange juice
2	tablespoons extra virgin olive oil
4½	teaspoons red wine vinegar
½	teaspoon finely minced fresh rosemary leaves (optional)
	Pinch of sea salt
½	teaspoon freshly ground black pepper

ROAST THE PEPPERS directly over the flame of a gas stove, turning occasionally, until the skins are charred and wrinkled. As an alternative, you can place the peppers on a jelly-roll pan and place under the broiler set on high, turning occasionally, until the skins are blistered and blackened all over. After the peppers are blackened, place them in either a plastic bag or a deep bowl covered with plastic wrap. Let cool for 20 minutes.

MEANWHILE, wash and trim the fennel stalks and delicate greenery. Discard the stalks, but reserve the foliage. Coarsely chop the greenery to make ⅓ cup. Slice off the bottom ½ inch of the bulb and discard. Slice the bulb into thin matchstick strips and separate.

WHISK TOGETHER the orange juice, olive oil, vinegar, rosemary, salt, and pepper. When the peppers have cooled, trim the stem ends and split the peppers open. Scrape off the charred skin with a knife, or rub with a nubby terry-cloth towel. Remove the seeds and stems and cut each pepper into 1-inch by 1-inch squares.

PLACE THE PEPPER SQUARES, fennel matchsticks, and fennel greenery into a mixing bowl, pour the vinaigrette over them, and toss. Allow 2 hours to marinate. Serve the salad at room temperature for fullest flavor.

Edward's Field Greens

SINCE THE 1970s, *I have kept a postcard framed on my desk. It is an Edward Gorey drawing of a well-turned-out Victorian couple being tossed higgledy-piggledy into the air along with an assortment of lettuce greens whirling in the air about them. The caption reads: "Life is a recipe-less salad that's forever being tossed." This salad is in homage to Mr. Gorey's sentiments, and it is, in fact, a recipe-less recipe. The ingredients here are merely a list of suggestions. We vary Edward's salad with seasonal availability of greens and intriguing fruit, nut, and herb combinations. Toss it up!*

Serves 4

SHALLOT VINAIGRETTE DRESSING

2   shallots, finely minced
2   tablespoons white wine vinegar
6   tablespoons walnut oil
    Zest of 1 orange
1/2 teaspoon kosher salt
1/2 teaspoon freshly ground black pepper

SALAD

1   pound assorted greens (such as mizuna, frisée, arugula, baby spinach, baby beet greens, oak leaf lettuces, baby romaine, tatsoi)
2   tablespoons finely minced flat-leaf parsley
8   fresh basil leaves, torn
2   sprigs thyme, leaves stripped and minced
2   sprigs fresh mint, leaves stripped and cut into julienne
4   fresh chives, finely minced
1/2 fresh pomegranate, seeded, or 2 star fruits, sliced into 1/8-inch stars, or 3 kumquats, sliced into very thin rounds
1/4 cup toasted whole hazelnuts, skins removed and coarsely chopped, or piñon nuts (pine nuts)

TO MAKE THE DRESSING, put all the ingredients in a small bowl and whisk with a wire balloon whisk until emulsified.

TO MAKE THE SALAD, toss it all together!

Epiphany Mango-Beet Salad

KITTY LEAKEN IS AN INTREPID PHOTOGRAPHER *whose work you see throughout this book. We once took a side trip to the Isthmus of Mexico during a photographic expedition to Oaxaca. We spent an unforgettable afternoon exploring the open-air market at Juchitan de Zaragoza. Kitty bought a bunch of beets and I bought baby mangoes, our respective favorite foods. I thought to myself, why not pair them up and toss them with the bright flavors of lime, orange, mint, and cayenne? The colors of this salad are tropically bright, reminding one of sun-drenched bougainvilleas. The flavor and beautiful color combination is simple and striking, a real epiphany!*

Serves 4

DRESSING

⅓ cup freshly squeezed orange juice
⅓ cup freshly squeezed lime juice
¼ teaspoon cayenne pepper
¼ teaspoon kosher salt

SALAD

6 large beets
3 ripe mangoes
½ cup whole macadamia nuts, for garnish
Pinch of kosher salt
4 cups field greens or arugula leaves
⅓ cup fresh mint leaves, stemmed and
　 cut into julienne, for garnish

TO MAKE THE DRESSING, put all the ingredients into a nonreactive bowl and whisk together.

TO MAKE THE SALAD, wash the beets and cut off their greens, leaving a 2-inch stem. (Reserve the beet greens for another use.) Steam the beets in a steamer over boiling water on top of the stove over high heat, or roast them, wrapped individually in foil, in a 400°F oven for 1½ hours, or until fork-tender by either method. When the beets have cooled, peel and cut them into ½-inch cubes and set aside in a bowl.

PREHEAT THE OVEN to 300°F. To dice the mangos it is necessary to cut the mango into two halves. Rest the mango on end on a cutting board, stem end up, with the narrow view facing you. Cut 1 inch on either side of the stem, cutting straight down to avoid the large oval-shaped pit in the center. Place the mango half flesh side up in the palm of your hand, and with the other hand use the tip of a paring knife to make ½-inch diagonal cuts going in opposite directions, creating an evenly spaced grid. Cut down deeply, but not through the mango skin. Turn the cut mango halves inside out and the still-attached squares will pop up like porcupine spines, ready for easy release by cutting each piece into a bowl. Repeat until all the mangoes are diced. After cutting away the halves, there will be plenty of juicy fruit left on the pits that will not be usable for dicing but that is great for the cook to slurp over the sink as a snack. Keep the mangos and beets separate until it is time to serve.

TOAST THE MACADAMIA NUTS in the preheated oven until golden brown, about 10 minutes. Stir occasionally. Let cool, then wrap the nuts in a dish towel. Use a heavy

skillet to smash the nuts, turning the towel a couple of times, to make a "crumble." Sprinkle with the salt.

ASSEMBLE THE SALAD just before serving. Put half of the dressing into a bowl, and use a set of tongs to toss the greens quickly, evenly dividing them among individual salad plates. Put the mangoes and beets into the same bowl. Gently and quickly combine them with the remaining dressing. Place the mixture on top of the greens and sprinkle on the mint and macadamia crumbs for garnish. The citrus dressing will make the greens wilt if allowed to stand, so serve immediately.

Kyra's Russian Potato Salad

"REMEMBER, LIFE'S A PICNIC NOT A NIT-PICK." —Effie Parsons

This Russian heirloom recipe was a gift from my dear friend Vanya Boestrom, whose mother, Kyra, made this for family picnics. Its texture is both crunchy and smooth, and its pink color and summer flavors will entice you to make it for your picnics again and again. The sweet beets and sour pickles are enlivened by fresh dill. Use a hand grater to grate the hard-boiled eggs; it's faster and there is little cleanup with this method, an innovation from the geniuses in our kitchen. Hold the egg against the grater with the flat of your hand to avoid nicking your fingers.

Serves 8

1 pound beets (canned shredded beets may be substituted)

3 pounds russet potatoes

4½ teaspoons kosher salt

¼ cup olive oil

1 teaspoon freshly ground black pepper

4 eggs, hard-boiled and peeled

3 dill pickles, finely diced (Clausens' brand is recommended)

4 green onions, green and white parts, finely sliced

½ cup minced fresh dill leaves

1 cup mayonnaise

PREHEAT THE OVEN to 400°F. Wash the beets and cut the leaves off, leaving 2 inches of the stems attached. (Reserve the nourishing leaves for another use.) Do not disturb the roots or peel the skin, as the color will bleed out. Tightly wrap each beet in foil and put in a roasting pan. Roast them in the oven for 1¼ hours, or until fork-tender. Cool, peel, and cut into ¼-inch cubes.

WHILE THE BEETS are cooking, peel the potatoes and place them in a large pot with 1 tablespoon of the salt and enough water to cover them. Boil until fork-tender. Drain and cool before cutting into ½-inch cubes. After the potatoes are cut, add the olive oil, remaining 1½ teaspoons of salt, and pepper and mix together.

GRATE 3 OF THE hard-boiled eggs, using the large holes on a box-style cheese grater, and set aside. Slice the remaining hard-boiled egg and set aside for garnish. In a large mixing bowl, put in the potatoes, beets, grated eggs, pickles, green onions, and ¼ cup of the dill. Add the mayonnaise and combine. (You may choose to add more.) Adjust the salt and pepper to taste. Chill well before serving. Garnish each serving with a slice of the reserved hard-boiled egg and sprinkle with the remaining ¼ cup of dill.

Grilled Pigs and Figs with Field Greens

A FRIEND OF MINE *once bit into one of these grilled bacon-wrapped figs. It was hot off the grill, the fig's summer sugars were caramelized from the fire, and the thick applewood-smoked bacon was crisp and fragrant. He did indeed inhale, then he tasted, chewed, swallowed, looked dazed, and then wept. Sit these creations atop some sassy greens tossed with balsamic vinegar, sprinkle on some Spanish cabrales (a blue cheese) for that salt thang, and you too could weep for the joy of it, the liveliest salad I know.*

Serves 4

SALAD

24	slices applewood-smoked, thick-cut bacon
12	fresh black mission figs
6	cups salad greens mix
1/4	cup cabrales cheese, crumbled, for garnish

BALSAMIC VINEGAR DRESSING

2	tablespoons balsamic vinegar
6	tablespoons extra virgin olive oil
	Pinch of sea salt and
	freshly ground black pepper

PREHEAT THE OVEN to 300°F. Cover a jelly-roll pan with parchment paper (for easy cleanup). Lay out the bacon strips in the pan, put in the oven, and cook for 20 minutes, until the bacon begins to crisp but still maintains its flexibility. (If you are adept at cooking bacon in the microwave, cook it according to the manufacturer's instructions halfway to doneness, with paper towels on top and under it.) Drain the bacon and set aside.

PREHEAT THE GRILL. While the bacon cooks, whisk the dressing ingredients together in a salad bowl with a wire balloon whisk.

WRAP EACH FIG with 2 pieces of the partially cooked bacon, one around the circumference of the fig and one over the stem end and bottom of the fig. Secure the bacon with wooden toothpicks. Grill the figs over medium heat until the bacon is crispy and the figs are warmed through, about 10 minutes, turning with tongs as needed.

WASH, DRAIN, AND DRY the greens. Toss them with the dressing in the salad bowl and use a pair of tongs to turn the greens in the dressing until they are well coated.

DIVIDE THE GREENS equally among 4 serving plates and nestle the figs on top, 3 per plate, and then sprinkle the cabrales on top. Serve immediately with a box of facial tissue for those tears of joy.

Thai Squid Salad (Yam Pla Muek)

CHEF LAURA TAYLOR *cooked at the Cafe for many years. During that time, she also spent many months exploring and studying cuisine in Thailand. She now has her own restaurant, Superfine, in Brooklyn, New York. She sent me this recipe from her travels. It is at once sweet, spicy hot, comforting, and enlivening. If you do not already own one, now is the time to purchase a multilayer bamboo steamer to place over a pot or wok of boiling water. Have all preparations in place, because the cooking is rapid and the squid should be served hot, right after its 2 minutes of cooking time. Since your guests must be ready to eat this salad immediately, you may want to include them in the cooking drama. Tantalize them by letting them watch the rapid cooking and assembly.*

Serves 4

2 tablespoons fish sauce (nam pla)

2 tablespoons freshly squeezed lime juice

½ teaspoon sugar

2 green Thai chiles (serrano chiles may be substituted), stemmed, seeded, and finely minced

5 cloves garlic, finely minced

1 bunch cilantro, leaves and stems coarsely chopped

4 green onions, green and white parts, cut into ¼-inch slices

4 stalks celery heart, including the leaves, coarsely chopped

½ red onion, thinly sliced

6 cups Asian greens, alone or in combination: tatsoi, mizuna, Chinese cabbage, or field greens

1 pound fresh or frozen squid steaks

1 teaspoon red chile flakes (pequin)

1 bunch Thai basil, for garnish

PUT THE FISH SAUCE, lime juice, and sugar into a bowl and whisk until the sugar dissolves. Put the chiles, garlic, cilantro, green onions, celery, red onion, and mixed greens into a large bowl. Prepare a layered steamer and bring the water to a boil. Score the squid steaks with the tip of a sharp paring knife in a diagonal grid pattern, making the cuts ¼ inch apart.

PLACE THE SQUID in the steamer, making sure not to stack the squid steaks. By the clock, steam for exactly 2 minutes over boiling water. Toss the vegetables with the dressing, reserving 1 tablespoon of the dressing. Place the greens in a mound on separate serving plates, retrieve the squid, and place the steaks off center on the greens. Drizzle the reserved dressing over the squid and sprinkle the red chile flakes over all. Garnish with the Thai basil sprigs. Serve immediately.

Lunch

Baked Macaroni and Cheese

WE WERE THE ONLY FAMILY *in the casserole-crazed 1950s that had one—and only one—casserole recipe in the family repertoire, mostly because my brother John refused to eat what he called "squishy" food. This is not "squishy" mac and cheese; it is meant to be crispy on top, and it holds together so well that it is a snap to cut into portions and serve. At the Cafe we often add a layer of creamed spinach and cooked turkey bacon to the layers, so add some fillip of your own. As the casserole bakes, it fills the house with an aroma that will create hunger pangs. Be prepared to serve this ever-popular indulgence as soon as it is out of the oven.*

Serves 6

5	teaspoons sea salt
1	pound elbow macaroni or cavatappi (corkscrew) pasta
6	tablespoons (¾ stick) unsalted butter
4	poblano chiles (optional)
1¼	pounds extra-sharp aged Cheddar cheese, grated
3	tablespoons prepared yellow mustard
2	teaspoons freshly ground black pepper
3	cups whole milk
2	pinches of paprika

FILL A LARGE STOCKPOT with water, add 3 teaspoons of the sea salt, and bring to a boil over high heat. Add the pasta and boil for 8 minutes. Check for doneness and drain in a colander.

PREHEAT THE OVEN to 375°F. Grease a 9-inch by 13-inch glass baking dish with 1 tablespoon of the butter, leaving any extra bits divided among the four corners of the pan.

ROAST THE POBLANO CHILES over an open flame under a broiler, or grill on the stove top until blackened all over, turning with tongs to ensure even blackening. Let the chiles "sweat" in a plastic bag for 10 minutes, or until they are cool enough to handle. Stem and peel by scraping with a knife or rubbing in a terry-cloth towel, then scrape out the seeds and cut the chiles into thin strips. Set aside.

TO ASSEMBLE THE CASSEROLE, place one-third of the cooked pasta in the baking dish and sprinkle on one-third of the remaining 2 teaspoons of salt and one-third of the cheese. Smooth on 1 tablespoon of the mustard, then lay half of the chile strips over all. Scatter bits of one-third of the remaining 5 tablespoons of butter, then sprinkle on one-third of the black pepper. Repeat the process for the next two layers.

AFTER THE PASTA, salt, cheese, mustard, butter, and black pepper have been spread onto the third layer, pour the milk over the casserole, then evenly sprinkle the pinches of paprika over the top. Bake for 1 hour, or until the top layer is crispy and brown. Serve hot from the oven on warmed plates.

Carne Asada with Berbere Spice

THIS SUCCULENT NEW MEXICAN DISH *is improved by using an Ethiopian spice blend called berbere, also known as peri peri. It is a combination of ground ginger, cinnamon, fenugreek, cardamom, coriander, and red pepper. Carne asada means "grilled meat" in Spanish. We used to prepare the asada in the traditional manner by spicing the meat exclusively with red chile powder, but berbere really sparks this old standby. Try berbere on steak as a rub before grilling, or on chicken before baking, or on pork ribs before roasting. We make it available for sale at the Cafe and on our web site. It can also, of course, be obtained from African markets (see page 147).*

Try to obtain a cut of beef called the loin flap, which is cut from the underside of the ribs. Sometimes, butchers call this cut "fajita meat," but always ask and find out whether it is indeed from the loin flap. Flank steak can also be used, as can skirt steak, but it's just not as delicious, so be a hunter-gatherer and make an effort to find this preferred cut. As with all meat selections, always make the effort to find hormone-free, organically fed, free-range raised beef. If you don't already own a meat pounder for tenderizing meats, purchase an inexpensive, handy, jaccard-style bladed tenderizer from a kitchen shop. It has sharp teeth that tenderize with a row of sixteen separate blades, stamping into the meat in a rapid stabbing motion. Needless to say, it is the most effective tool for this purpose.

At the Cafe, we serve this dish with sides of black beans, guacamole, grilled red onion pieces, grilled poblano chiles, and, of course, warmed corn tortillas.

Serves 4

¾ cup olive oil

1 tablespoon berbere spice

1½ tablespoons pressed garlic

½ cup freshly squeezed lime juice

½ red onion, diced

1½ teaspoons kosher salt

1 teaspoon freshly ground black pepper

2 pounds beef loin flap, pounded on both sides, each piece cut into 1½-inch by 3-inch strips

2 limes, cut into wedges, for garnish

IN A LARGE GLASS or stainless steel bowl, whisk together the oil, berbere, garlic, lime juice, onion, salt, and pepper. Add the beef and mix thoroughly. Cover with plastic wrap to seal. Marinate the meat in the refrigerator for at least 4 hours or up to 24 hours.

PREPARE A CHARCOAL or gas grill. When the grill is ready, cook the meat about 6 inches from the medium-hot fuel. Turn after 1 minute and cook for another 2 minutes so that the meat remains juicy and slightly pink. Serve immediately with lime wedges and desired accompaniments.

Chorizo Quiche with Cornmeal Crust

CHORIZO IS MEXICAN SAUSAGE, *not to be confused with the chorizo from Spain that is less spicy and made with smoked pork, whereas Mexican chorizo is made with fresh pork. (For the Mexican chorizo recipe, see page 5.) This quiche recipe comes out of the oven pretty as a picture. There is a perfect flavor balance between the spiciness of the chorizo and the sweetness of the eggs and cornmeal crust. Served with a green salad, this recipe will make feeding a crowd a cinch.*

Serves 6

CRUST

1	cup all-purpose flour
½	cup cornmeal
½	cup unsalted butter
1	large organic egg
1	egg yolk
1	teaspoon ice water, plus more if needed

CHORIZO FILLING

3	large organic eggs, beaten
1½	cups heavy cream
8	ounces chorizo sausage, crumbled and uncooked
½	cup chopped green onions, green and white parts
1	cup shredded Monterey Jack cheese
¼	teaspoon cayenne pepper

TO MAKE THE CRUST, lightly butter a glass baking dish 9 inches in diameter by 2½ inches high. Put the flour, cornmeal, and butter into the bowl of a food processor fitted with a steel blade. Process in short bursts until it has the consistency of small peas. Add in the egg and egg yolk and process again for a moment. Turn this mixture out onto a work surface and add in just as much ice water as it takes to work the dough into a firm ball.

FLOUR YOUR WORK SURFACE and a rolling pin. Roll out the dough until it is ⅛ inch thick and fit it into the glass dish. Crimp the edges of the dough and refrigerate the crust for at least 20 minutes before baking to allow the gluten in the dough to relax. Prepare the filling while the crust chills.

TO MAKE THE FILLING, preheat the oven to 400°F. Put the eggs and the heavy cream into a bowl and whisk together. Add the chorizo and green onions and whisk again.

PREHEAT THE CRUST for 5 minutes, then sprinkle the bottom of the shell with half of the cheese. Pour the filling mixture over it and top with the rest of the cheese. Sprinkle the top with the cayenne pepper. Bake for about 40 minutes, until the custard is set, the top is a light golden color, and a knife inserted into the center comes out clean. Allow for about 30 minutes of cooling time. Serve while still warm.

Green Chile Sauce with Dried Green Chiles

THIS IS THE UBIQUITOUS SAUCE *of New Mexican cuisine. It is used on breakfast eggs, enchiladas, and burritos. With the addition of meats and vegetables, it is also used in stews. This version of green chile sauce uses dried chiles that conveniently come in 1-ounce packages, available from the Cafe's shop (see page 147). You may also purchase frozen prepared green chiles that are already roasted, peeled, and chopped. The frozen ones, however, do not have the smoky roasted flavor of the dried chiles. If those two options are unavailable, try to obtain fresh New Mexican green chiles that resemble Anaheim chiles. Failing that, Anaheim chiles may be substituted, but they are very mild and could be augmented with 1 or 2 poblanos, jalapeños, or serranos if more heat is desired. The sauce may be kept in the refrigerator for up to 4 days and frozen for up to 2 months.*

Capsaicin is the chemical found in all chiles that, when eaten, releases stress hormones in the body, speeds up metabolism, and gives a distinct sensation of well-being. In New Mexico, we call this phenomena the "chile fix!" Be sure to wear gloves when handling chiles if you are sensitive to them, and don't rub your eyes with hands that have touched chiles. The best antidote for eating a chile that is too hot for comfort is to down a few swallows of milk or eat any sort of dairy product until the pain subsides. Some swear that a tablespoon of sugar or honey is the best panacea. This recipe, however, is not a hurt'n chile sauce at all.

Makes 4 cups

1   ounce dried green chiles, or 1½ pounds fresh mild green New Mexican chiles plus ¾ pound hot New Mexican green chiles, or 2 cups frozen green chiles

4   cups water

½   white onion, cut into medium-size cubes

6   cloves garlic, finely diced

2   teaspoons dried Mexican oregano or dried marjoram leaves

1½ teaspoons kosher salt

2   tablespoons vegetable oil

3   tablespoons all-purpose flour

TO HYDRATE THE DRIED GREEN CHILES, pour boiling water over them and let them soak for 30 minutes. Drain the chiles. Remove any peels that may be present, then slice into ¼-inch strips and cut into ½-inch cubes.

IF USING FRESH CHILES, roast them over an open flame on a grill, or lay the chiles directly on the burners of a gas stove on high heat. Turn the chiles with tongs until they are charred and blistered all over. You may also opt to put the chiles in a flameproof pan under the broiler of a stove. Use tongs to turn them often, ensuring that the whole chile is charred. Put the chiles immediately into a plastic bag or inside a cotton cloth towel and wrap tightly to let the chiles "sweat." Let them steam for at least 10 minutes. When cool enough to handle, peel the chiles, slit them open, and remove the seeds and veins.

(Do not use water to peel the roasted chiles because the caramelized flavors will be washed away.) Chop them and measure out 2 cups.

PUT EITHER TYPE of the now-prepared chiles, along with the water, onion, garlic, oregano, and salt into a saucepan and barely simmer, uncovered, over low heat for 20 minutes. Meanwhile, put the oil into a small saucepan over low heat and heat for 1 minute. Add the flour, stirring with a wire balloon whisk, until the roux becomes light golden in color and gives off a nutlike aroma. Add ½ cup of the green chile mixture to the roux and stir vigorously to incorporate. Add the roux mixture to the saucepan holding the rest of the green chile sauce, stir to mix, and simmer for 15 minutes. Adjust the taste for additional salt and store the sauce in a nonreactive covered container if not serving immediately. When reheating, be sure to heat the sauce slowly over low heat and stir frequently, because it is easily scorched. Consider reheating by using a microwave to avoid scorching.

Green Chile and Pork Stew

THIS IS THE CLASSIC *thick stew of northern New Mexico, but of course there are as many recipes as there are Norteños (northerners). This recipe is from my dear friend Greg Powell, a native son of Santa Fe, whose palate is unsurpassed. Lamb, chicken, or game may be used for the meat—whatever is on hand is fine to use. There is a lot of chopping and dicing, as well as a long cooking process, so be prepared for about a 4-hour commitment that will give you a delicious and nourishing reward for your effort, not to mention the sweet cooking aromas that will fill your kitchen. The quantity given is large, because the cooking time is long and it only seems fair to create extra. It freezes well and may be kept for up to 2 months. Use the best quality pork butt you can find.*

Makes 12 servings

¼ cup olive oil

2 yellow onions, diced

4 carrots, peeled and diced

4 stalks celery, diced

4 cloves garlic, pressed

1 teaspoon dried oregano

1 tablespoon ground cumin

2 pounds pork butt

5 quarts chicken stock (you can get low-sodium, organic stock in quart cartons from the grocery, or use the recipe on page 27)

1 cup fresh corn kernels, cut from 1 to 2 ears of corn

3 pounds russet potatoes, cut into 1-inch chunks (no need to peel)

16 fresh New Mexican or Anaheim chiles, fire-roasted, stemmed, peeled, seeded, and cut into ½-inch squares (2 cups), or 1 ounce dried green chiles, rehydrated and chopped (see Sources, page 147)

¾ teaspoon sea salt

1 teaspoon freshly ground black pepper

12 corn or whole-wheat tortillas, warmed

IN A LIDDED, 8-quart, heavy pot, over medium heat, add the olive oil and let it heat for a moment. To the pot add the onion, carrots, celery, garlic, and oregano. Sauté the vegetables, uncovered, until the onions are translucent. Put the cumin into a dry pan over low heat and toast it for 1 minute, stirring frequently until it is fragrant, and then add it to the stew pot. Cut the pork in half and add it to the pot, followed by 3 quarts of the stock. Cover the pot, bring to a boil, uncover, skim off any foam, and then turn down the heat to medium-low. Simmer gently, uncovered, over medium-low heat until the meat is tender, about 2½ to 3 hours. (You may need to add 1 quart of the remaining stock at this point if too much has evaporated.)

TRANSFER THE PORK to a bowl, leaving the stock in the pot. Skim any oil from the top of the stock and discard. When the meat is cool enough to handle, shred the meat, then coarsely chop it with a cleaver so the shreds are no more than 2 inches long. Return the meat to the stockpot and add the corn, potatoes, chiles, and the remaining 1 quart of stock. Cook until the potatoes are fork-tender, about 30 minutes. Add the salt and pepper. Always serve this stew with warmed tortillas.

Grilled Squash and Red Onion Enchilada with Red or Green Chile Sauce

SMOKY GRILLED FLAVORS *make this the quintessential enchilada. We serve this popular dish in the traditional New Mexican "flat" enchilada style. The tortillas are not rolled; instead, the enchilada is assembled in layers. You can use boiled and shredded chicken here in place of the vegetables. Also in the tradition of northern New Mexican cuisine, you may serve 1 or 2 fried eggs right on top, for a protein-enriched embellishment. If you get ambitious enough to prepare both the red and the green chile sauces, or have them on hand in the refrigerator or freezer, they can be ladled over the enchiladas in half portions, as native New Mexicans frequently do. When the enchilada (or any other chile-laden dish) has red sauce over one half and green over the other, the style is appropriately referred to as "Christmas."*

Serves 4

1	cup vegetable oil or low-sodium organic chicken stock (page 27)
8	corn tortillas
½	pound red onion (1⅓ cups), cut into thin round slices
1	pound zucchini (3 cups), ends trimmed and cut into ¼-inch-thick diagonal slices
4	cups grated Monterey Jack cheese
4	cups red chile or green chile sauce, or 2 cups of each (see page 76 for the red sauce, and page 66 for the green sauce)
8	corn or whole-wheat tortillas, warmed

PREHEAT A GRILL. Put the oil into a sauté pan over medium heat, and when the oil is warmed, using tongs, slip each tortilla in turn into the oil. Flip each tortilla after 15 seconds. Remove the tortilla when just heated through and still floppy. Drain any excess oil from the tortilla over the pan. Place the finished tortilla on paper towels and keep warm. Repeat until all are softened. (A healthier way of softening the tortilla is to use tongs to dip it into simmering chicken stock for a few seconds, and then drain on paper towels.)

COOK THE ONIONS and zucchini on the grill until the onions are a bit blackened and the zucchini is just tender. If no grill is available, cover the bottom of a large sauté pan with olive oil and sauté the onions and zucchini over medium heat. Cook the vegetables until the onions are translucent and the zucchini just tender.

PREHEAT THE BROILER, being sure to adjust the wire shelf to accommodate the enchiladas once they are assembled. The cheese needs a close heat source in order to melt.

TO ASSEMBLE, place 1 cooked tortilla on each of 4 heat-proof serving plates. Equally divide the vegetables, half the cheese, and half the chile sauce of your choice, then top with another tortilla and the rest of the cheese and sauce. Place each plate under the broiler in turn until the cheese has melted and is bubbling. Serve immediately with warmed corn or whole-wheat tortillas on the side.

Chinese Hacked Chicken

THIS SPICY CHICKEN *dish is "cooled" by being wrapped in lettuce and eaten with your hands. It makes a perfect summer lunch when arranged on individual plates or presented on a showy platter for buffets, or serve it as an hors d'oeuvre with drinks. (It is a bit addicting, so forewarned is forearmed.)*

Serves 4

1½	pounds boneless, skinless, organic chicken breasts
⅓	cup peanut oil
1	tablespoon Szechuan peppercorns or mixed red, green, black, and white peppercorns
6	tablespoons smooth-style organic peanut butter
3	tablespoons toasted sesame oil
3	tablespoons organic soy sauce
3	tablespoons rice wine vinegar
2¼	teaspoons cayenne pepper
2½	teaspoons crushed red pepper flakes
2	tablespoons grated fresh ginger
2	tablespoons minced garlic
3	green onions, green and white parts, finely sliced
2	heads Boston (butter or Bibb) lettuce leaves, separated, washed, and dried
18	cilantro sprigs, for garnish

IN A LARGE SAUCEPAN, poach the chicken in simmering water for 5 minutes or until cooked through. Drain, cool, and shred into 3-inch strips, ¼ inch wide. Set aside.

PLACE THE PEANUT OIL in a small saucepan and add the peppercorns. Bring the oil up to a simmer (300° F) and roast the peppercorns for 5 minutes, or until the oil is fragrant. Strain and discard the peppercorns. Combine the peanut butter, sesame oil, and peanut oil in a mixing bowl and stir together until smooth. Add the soy sauce, vinegar, cayenne, red pepper flakes, ginger, garlic, and green onions. Stir to combine. Add the shredded chicken and mix until well incorporated. Refrigerate until serving time.

DIVIDE THE CHICKEN and lettuce leaves evenly among individual plates. Garnish with cilantro for inclusion in the wrap. Instruct your guests to top the lettuce leaves with a spoonful of chicken, then wrap it into a bundle and eat it with their hands, like a "lettuce burrito."

LEFT: Day chef Gabriel Ruiz in the order kitchen

Napo's El Salvadoran Tamal in Banana Leaf

THIS IS, FOR MY TASTE BUDS, *the quintessential tamal experience. The rich flavors will beguile the most jaded of palates. We employ an added note by using Iroquois white corn flour that is roasted before it is ground, which adds an amazing depth of flavor and fragrance (see Sources, page 148). Achiote paste is made from the seed of the annatto plant and lends a deep, earthy quality to the flavor. Achiote is readily available from Latin markets (see Sources, page 147). A package of banana leaves is usually available frozen from most Latin or Asian markets. You will also need a stacking steamer or a large covered pot with a steamer basket to keep the boiling water away from the tamales.*

Makes 12 tamales

SALSA ROJO

1 ancho chile, stemmed and torn into pieces
¼ cup sesame seeds
¼ cup hulled pumpkin seeds
1 pinch of ground allspice
1 pinch of paprika
1 teaspoon ground cumin
4 tomatoes, cored and cut into quarters
1 stalk celery, thinly sliced
1 clove garlic, coarsely chopped
1 tablespoon achiote paste
1 teaspoon salt
1 pinch freshly ground black pepper
½ cup water
¼ cup olive oil

MASA

4 cups roasted Iroquois white corn flour
2 tablespoons olive oil
½ teaspoon salt
½ teaspoon pepper
1 teaspoon ground cumin

½ cup (1 stick) unsalted butter
3 quarts vegetable stock (store-bought organic is fine)

FILLING

2 tablespoons olive oil
1 zucchini, trimmed and grated
¾ pound red potatoes, peeled
1 package banana leaves, thawed
¾ cup grated asadero or Monterey Jack cheese (12 ounces)
2 poblano chiles, roasted, peeled, stemmed, seeded, and cut into ¼-inch strips

TO MAKE THE SALSA, heat a dry skillet over low heat, and put in the chile, sesame seeds, pumpkin seeds, allspice, paprika, and cumin. Toast the ingredients, stirring, until they are fragrant, about 3 minutes. Remove from the heat. Put the toasted spices and all the remaining salsa ingredients into the bowl of a food processor or the container of a blender and whirl until well incorporated. Set aside.

TO MAKE THE MASA, put all the ingredients into a large saucepan and cook over very low heat, uncovered, for

30 minutes, stirring frequently to prevent sticking. Remove from the heat and set aside.

TO MAKE THE FILLING, warm the olive oil in a sauté pan and lightly sauté the grated zucchini, uncovered, for 4 minutes over medium heat. Boil the potatoes in a saucepan with enough boiling water to cover, until just fork-tender. Let cool, then cut into 12 pieces. Set both the zucchini and the potatoes aside, along with the other filling ingredients.

TO ASSEMBLE THE TAMAL, cut the banana leaves into 12 rectangles measuring 9 inches by 11 inches. Make 12 strips of banana leaves ¼ inch wide for ties. For each tamal, place ½ cup of masa in the center of a banana leaf

in a rectangle about 2 inches by 3 inches. On top of the masa place 2 tablespoons of the salsa, 1 tablespoon of the cheese, 3 or 4 of the chile strips, 1 tablespoon of zucchini, and lastly a piece of potato.

TO WRAP THE TAMAL, fold the sides of each leaf up and over the middle of the filling and then fold each end toward the middle, overlapping the ends. Tie the package with a strip of leaf so that the ends are secured and the knot is on top of the smooth side of the tamal.

STEAM THE TAMALES in a steamer pot, covered, over boiling water for 1¼ hours, checking to replenish the boiling water as necessary. Serve piping hot.

ABOVE: Our cooks, the charismatic brothers, Daniel, Jesus, and Pablo Rivera Landeverde

Pasqual's Preferred Red Chile Sauce

THIS RED CHILE SAUCE, *contributed by chef Martin Wright, is used consistently in all our enchiladas, burritos, and bowls of chile and beans. It can also add zip to many soups. Imported Mexican-grown dried chiles are noted for their fruity and rich flavors, especially when used in combination. When purchasing dried peppers, keep in mind that they should be bright in color and pliable. Avoid brittle, yellowed, or pale chiles.*

Makes 4 cups

1	quart water
16	guajillo chiles, stemmed and seeded
8	ancho chiles, stemmed and seeded
4	chiles de arbol, stemmed
2	cloves garlic
1	tablespoon red wine vinegar
1	teaspoon dried oregano
½	white onion, coarsely chopped
1	tablespoon kosher salt

IN A SAUCEPAN large enough to hold all the ingredients, bring the water to a boil. Add all the ingredients, return to a boil, and cook for 5 minutes, covered, over high heat. Remove from the heat and let cool completely before blending. Place the mixture into the container of a blender and whirl until smooth. Strain through a China cap strainer or other large wire-mesh strainer. Discard the seeds. Adjust the salt and refrigerate, covered, until ready to use. Red chile sauce may be held in the refrigerator for up to 5 days and in the freezer for 2 months.

Reuben Sandwich

WE LIKE TO THINK *at the Cafe that we have perfected this essential sandwich. For those of us who believe that a great corned beef on rye can solve all the problems of the world (or at least our own), there is an instant connoisseurship that is bestowed by the sandwich gods on us cognoscenti. One great twist to this recipe, given to me by generous chef George Dimsey, is to mellow the flavor of the sauerkraut by simmering it in white wine. Eureka! Our former pastry chef Elizabeth Quirante is a vegetarian, so she invented the tofu variation, which is also quite delicious and popular at the Cafe. Purchase sauerkraut that is packaged in a jar or plastic pouch, and avoid the canned variety. Imported Gruyère cheese is best by far.*

Makes 4 sandwiches

PASQUAL'S RUSSIAN DRESSING

- ½ cup mayonnaise
- ¼ cup ketchup
- 1 tablespoon minced chives
- 2 large pitted green olives, minced
- ½ fresh poblano chile, stemmed, seeded, and finely chopped, to equal 2 tablespoons
- 1 hard-boiled egg, peeled and grated on a cheese grater

SANDWICH

- 2 cups sauerkraut
- ⅔ cup white wine
- 4 teaspoons softened butter
- 8 slices rye bread
- 1 pound thinly sliced, naturally raised, cooked corned beef or 1 pound firm tofu
- 2 cups grated Gruyère cheese

TO MAKE THE DRESSING, combine all the ingredients in a bowl and cover. Keep refrigerated until ready to use.

TO MAKE THE SANDWICH, preheat the broiler. Place the sauerkraut and wine into a medium saucepan and bring to a boil. Reduce the heat to a simmer and cook for 10 minutes. Drain the sauerkraut and keep warm.

BUTTER EACH SIDE of the bread slices with ½ teaspoon of butter and place them on a foil-covered baking sheet. Toast each side under the broiler until nicely toasted.

SPREAD ONE SIDE of each slice of toast with 2 tablespoons of the dressing. Set 4 of the toasted and slathered slices aside. Place ¼ pound of the corned beef on each of the remaining 4 toast slices and top each with ½ cup of sauerkraut and ½ cup of cheese. Return them to the broiler until the cheese is bubbling and browned. Place the reserved toast slices on top of the cheese (dressing side down, of course), and press the sandwiches together. Slice in half on the diagonal and serve immediately with plenty of napkins.

FOR THE TOFU VARIATION: Slice the tofu into 4 equal slabs and then cut on the diagonal. Heat a little olive oil in a nonstick sauté pan and sauté the tofu over medium heat until golden brown. Turn and brown the other side. Proceed with the assembly directions above.

Appetizers

Shrimp Boats with Guacamole and Chips

THESE CLEVERLY DESIGNED *little banana leaf pleated boats of shrimp, guacamole, and chips come from chef Napoleon Lopez, who cooked evenings at the Cafe for more than fifteen years. He brought this marvelous recipe from his hometown in El Salvador. These are terrific individual starter tastes, mixing the sweetness of shrimp and guacamole with the smoky heat of chipotle and chile powder.*

Serves 6

2	chipotle chiles en adobo
½	cup water
¼	cup medium-hot ground red chile powder
2	tablespoons olive oil
1	tablespoon freshly squeezed lime juice
½	teaspoon kosher salt
18	large shrimp, peeled, tails intact, and deveined
2	cups vegetable oil
12	fresh corn tortillas, cut into quarters
1	pinch sea salt
6	banana leaves, thawed and cut into 5-inch by 11-inch rectangles
3	cups guacamole (page 97)

PLACE THE CHILES EN ADOBO, water, chile powder, olive oil, lime juice, and kosher salt into a blender and puree until smooth. Put the shrimp into a nonreactive medium-sized bowl and pour the marinade over them. Stir to coat the shrimp evenly, cover, and refrigerate for at least 1 hour or up to 4 hours.

PLACE THE VEGETABLE OIL into a deep, straight-sided large saucepan over medium-high heat. Bring the oil to 360°F. Fry the cut tortillas until golden brown, turning once. Drain on paper towels, sprinkle with sea salt, and set aside.

PREHEAT A CHARCOAL or gas grill. Start preparing the banana leaf boats by cutting 1 dozen ½-inch by 5-inch strips for tying the ends of the banana leaf boats. (To visualize the banana boats, you must understand that the individual leaves are first pleated lengthwise and each end is tied tightly with the precut strip of banana leaf, then the pleated boat is opened out and downward to accommodate the guacamole, shrimp, and chips.) Place the 5-inch by 11-inch cut leaves the long way in front of you. Take one end of the leaf and pleat it lengthwise. Gather the end nearest you and tie it by wrapping the tie strip twice around the end of the "canoe," then make a knot. Turn the other end toward you and repeat. Open up the pleated leaf to make a canoe-shaped boat. Repeat to make the fleet.

REMOVE THE SHRIMP from the marinade and grill over high heat, turning once with tongs, until the shrimp are bright pink and no longer translucent in appearance. Do not overcook, because they will dry out and be tough. Let cool.

PLACE ½ CUP OF GUACAMOLE into each boat and poke in 3 shrimp tails so they stand upright. Place 4 fried corn tortillas between the shrimp and put each boat on individual serving plates. Serve immediately with a scattering of the remaining chips alongside the canoes.

Cheddar and Poppy Seed Bread Sticks

THESE ARE THE TASTIEST *and most delicate bread sticks that I know of. Every evening at dinner we place these bread sticks in a Mexican handblown glass cylinder at the center of each table, to welcome guests with a bite so they can settle in. You will need to have parchment paper on hand. The dough may be made a day in advance of baking, if it is tightly wrapped with plastic wrap for storage in the refrigerator. We use a multi-wheel-bladed cutter, which makes it easy to cut the dough into skinny sticks. Use orange-colored Cheddar cheese for the best effect.*

Makes 3 dozen bread sticks

2	tablespoons (¼ stick) unsalted butter
8	ounces extra-sharp Cheddar cheese, grated
1	large organic egg
2	tablespoons heavy cream
1⅛	cups all-purpose flour
1	tablespoon poppy seeds
½	teaspoon medium-hot chile powder

PREHEAT THE OVEN to 350°F. Put the butter and cheese into the bowl of an electric mixer. Use the paddle attachment to combine. When well incorporated, scrape the paddle attachment and replace with the dough hook attachment. Add the egg and mix, then add the heavy cream and mix again to combine all. With the machine running on low, slowly add the flour, then the poppy seeds and chile powder. Leave the mixer on for 15 minutes, until the dough is smooth and elastic.

REMOVE THE DOUGH from the mixer and knead by hand on a floured surface for 1 minute. Re-flour the work surface and roll the dough into a log shape, then flatten the log. Flour the work surface again. Use a floured rolling pin to roll the dough into a large rec-

tangle 12 inches by 16 inches by ¼ inch thick. Trim the edges with a pizza cutter to make them straight, then cut strips lengthwise ½ inch in width.

PLACE PARCHMENT PAPER on 3 baking sheets and carefully transfer the bread sticks, 12 to each pan. Bake for 20 minutes, until the sticks are just slightly browned. Remove and let cool completely before carefully transferring the sticks to a serving container.

Chile de Arbol Salsa

THIS VERSATILE SALSA *will find its way onto all sorts of foods once you cozy up to it. It's brilliant on tacos, egg dishes, rellenos, or quesadillas, or just with tortilla chips. It's essential with beef or lamb barbecoa.*

Makes 3 cups

3	chiles de arbol, stemmed
2	guajillo chiles, stemmed and seeded
1	jalapeño, stemmed and seeded
3	tomatoes, cored and cut into wedges
5	tomatillos, husked and halved
¼	large white onion, coarsely chopped
3	cloves garlic, coarsely chopped
⅛	teaspoon ground cumin
⅛	teaspoon dried oregano leaves
⅛	teaspoon ground cinnamon
⅛	teaspoon ground cloves
¾	teaspoon kosher salt
2¼	cups water

PUT ALL THE INGREDIENTS into a large saucepan. Bring to a boil, then lower the heat and simmer for 20 minutes. Put the mixture into the container of a blender, then cover the lid and container of the blender with a large dish towel. (The dish towel is a safety device; in case the lid is not tight enough, the towel will protect you from hot splashes when the blender is in operation.) Whirl until blended. Strain only if serving with barbecoa (page 108). Chill and serve as an appetizer with tortilla chips or as an accompaniment to the dishes listed above.

Verduras en Escabèche

VERDURAS EN ESCABÈCHE means "pickled vegetables" in Spanish. In Mexico, it is often served at the beginning of a meal, prepared in large pieces so that it may be picked up easily with the fingers. This El Salvadoran version is slaw-style. We serve this with pupusas (page 102).

Serves 4

2   carrots, peeled and cut into 1-inch chunks on
    the diagonal or 2 inches long in julienne

2   jalapeños, stemmed, seeded, and
    cut into julienne

2   cups shredded green cabbage

1   small beet, steamed over boiling water until
    fork-tender, peeled, and cut into julienne

1   small white onion, sliced into 8 pieces

3   tablespoons white vinegar

2   cups water, or to cover

$1\frac{1}{2}$ teaspoons dried Mexican oregano
    or dried marjoram

4   chiles de arbol, stemmed and crushed

1   teaspoon kosher salt

2   teaspoons sugar

TOSS ALL THE INGREDIENTS together and marinate overnight in the refrigerator, covered. Drain the mixture before serving.

Fresh Corn Cake

THIS FRESH CORN CAKE *gets its inspiration from Elizabeth Lambert Ortiz. We serve wedges of these daily and are constantly asked for the recipe. There's no reason that you couldn't make your own signature with this by adding minced chile, cheese, bacon, or nuts. Rice flour is available from health food supermarkets. Let yourself go, and have fun!*

Serves 8

½ cup (1 stick) unsalted butter
½ cup sugar
¼ cup whole milk
¼ cup heavy cream
7 to 8 cups corn kernels (cut from about 9 ears)
5 large organic eggs
¾ cup all-purpose flour
¾ cup rice flour
1 tablespoon baking powder
1 teaspoon kosher salt

PREHEAT THE OVEN to 350°F. Butter a round 9-inch cake pan, line the bottom with wax paper (cutting it to the same dimensions as the pan), then butter the paper. (Vegetable spray may be used on the pan instead of wax paper.)

PUT THE BUTTER into the bowl of an electric mixer with the paddle attachment and beat until creamy, about 5 minutes. Add the sugar and beat for another 3 minutes. Remove the bowl from the mixer and set aside.

SCALD THE MILK and heavy cream together in a small saucepan. Add the corn kernels, place the mixture into the container of a blender, and puree. Set aside and let cool.

SEPARATE THE EGG YOLKS and whites, reserving the whites. In a bowl, beat the egg yolks thoroughly with a whisk. Add the corn puree to the butter and sugar mixture, and then the egg yolks.

IN A MEDIUM BOWL, sift together the all-purpose flour, rice flour, baking powder, and salt. Mix this by hand into the wet ingredients. Transfer the batter to a large bowl.

WASH AND DRY the electric mixer bowl thoroughly. Fit the electric mixer with the wire whisk attachment and beat the egg whites until they form soft peaks. Use a rubber spatula to gently fold them into the batter.

SPOON THE BATTER into the prepared pan and bake for 45 minutes, or until golden brown. The corn cake should be set in the middle, so that a knife inserted into the center comes out clean. Let cool. To free the corn cake from the pan, run a knife around the edge and invert it onto a plate held over the top, serving side down. Flip the corn cake quickly and remove the wax paper. Heat to serve. Be sure to refrigerate any leftovers.

Fundido with Chorizo and Tortilla Chips

ASADERO IS A WHITE *cow's-milk cheese used for melting. Its name means "roaster." It is also known as queso Oaxaca or Chihuahua. It can be found in any Latin grocery or large supermarket. The addition of chorizo and scallions makes this a fiesta dip that will circle up any group* muy pronto. *Fry your own toasted tortilla chips. They will be sturdy enough to scoop the cheese and are far more satisfying than commercially made chips, especially since you can control the amount of salt to suit your taste. When completely cooled, the frying oil may be poured through a paper filter into a glass jar and reused. Note that some people are highly allergic to peanut or other nut oils, so inquire about your guests' dietary needs.*

Serves 4

1   quart peanut oil or other favorite frying oil

18 corn tortillas, cut into quarters

2   pinches of sea salt

2   ounces Mexican-style loose chorizo, removed from any casing

10 ounces asadero cheese, thinly sliced

2   green onions, white and green parts, sliced into thin rounds

IN A LARGE, DEEP-SIDED saucepan, heat the oil to 360°F. Fry the tortillas in batches and drain on paper towels. Sprinkle with sea salt. (You can make these a few hours ahead of serving.)

IN A SMALL SAUTÉ PAN, cook the chorizo over medium heat until browned, stirring frequently. Drain the chorizo of any liquid fat. Cover the bottom of a small, shallow, ovenproof serving dish with the cheese. Heat under the broiler until the cheese is bubbling and blistered. Remove from the broiler, smooth on the chorizo to cover, and return to the broiler for 3 more minutes. Remove and garnish with the scallions. Serve immediately with the tortilla chips. The cheese will be stringy, so have napkins at the ready.

Ghia-Pakora

THIS EAST INDIAN TREAT *celebrates the vegetable in golden bundles of chickpea flour. Chickpea flour, also known as garbanzo bean flour, is readily available in health food supermarkets. Be sure to allow yourself a lot of preparation time, because the vegetables need to "sweat" for 1 to 2 hours before cooking. Do not limit yourself on choice of vegetables: you may want to add simply slivered fresh ginger or carrots, or you may want to clean out the crisper drawer of your refrigerator with whatever that yields. The main thing is to keep the vegetables about the same size so that they cook at the same rate. The batter needs to sit for 20 minutes before it is fried. Serve these gems piping hot with fragrantly spiced tomato chutney (page 104) and collect your well-deserved oohs and ahhs.*

Makes 6 servings

6 medium zucchini, ends trimmed
    and cut into julienne
3 Japanese eggplant, cut into ¼-inch julienne
2 yellow onions, sliced into 2-inch-long strips
2 bunches cilantro, including
    stems, coarsely chopped
2 tablespoons kosher salt
4 tablespoons coriander seeds
2 teaspoons cumin seeds
2 teaspoons cayenne pepper
6 cups chickpea flour
2 teaspoons baking powder

MIX THE ZUCCHINI, eggplant, onions, and cilantro in a large mixing bowl. Toss well with the salt, then place them in a colander, either in the sink or over a plate, and let them "sweat" for 1 to 2 hours to release their excess moisture.

PREPARE A DEEP-FAT FRYER with peanut oil or other preferred oil for high-heat frying and preheat to 375°F.

TOAST THE CORIANDER and cumin seeds in a dry skillet over low heat until fragrant; do not brown. Mix the seeds with the cayenne, flour, and baking powder, and then sift the dry mixture over the vegetables. The batter should be fairly dry and stiff. Let it sit for 20 to 30 minutes. Use a large metal mixing spoon or a ⅓-cup metal scoop to portion out the mixture. Gently spoon the clumps into the hot peanut oil and fry until golden brown. Remove and drain on paper towels. Serve immediately with tomato chutney.

Guacamole

THE INDISPENSABLE AVOCADO *always proves its worth in concert with its pals: the chile, onion, tomato, garlic, cilantro, and lime juice that are found in this classic recipe. An avocado is ripe when it gives with a bit of pressure. A Hass avocado is very dark in color and has a bumpy skin. In the kitchen at the Cafe, we halve them with a sharp knife from end to end and remove the pit by laying the blade across the pit and twisting it slightly, so that it comes right out onto the edge of the blade. When ready to take out the flesh, we insert a spoon between the skin and the flesh of the avocado and follow the contour. Serve with store-bought tortilla chips, or fry your own (page 93).*

Makes 3 cups

2   jalapeños
     Vegetable oil
3   large ripe Hass avocados
¼   white onion, diced
1   tomato, cored, seeded, and diced
2   cloves garlic, pressed
⅓   cup finely minced cilantro, stems included
2   tablespoons freshly squeezed lime juice
1   teaspoon salt

RUB THE JALAPEÑOS with a small amount of vegetable oil and roast them over a direct flame on the stove top or under the broiler, turning them with tongs until the skin blisters and bubbles on all sides. When completely blackened, seal them in a plastic bag to let them "sweat" for about 10 minutes. Split open the chiles and scrape out the seeds, discarding the seeds and the stems, then mince the chiles. (There is no need to peel these.)

CUT THE AVOCADOS in half and remove the pits. Scoop out the avocado flesh and place it in a medium bowl. Mash the avocado with a potato masher or fork until smooth, but with small chunks still visible. Stir in the onion, tomato, garlic, cilantro, lime juice, jalapeño, and salt. Mix well.

COVER BY PRESSING plastic wrap directly onto the guacamole, which will completely seal the guacamole so that it does not discolor from contact with oxygen. Refrigerate until ready to use, but bring to room temperature before serving.

Mexican Shrimp Cocktail

A TRIP TO THE BEACH *in Mexico demands the pleasure of a perfectly prepared, refreshing shrimp cocktail. The genius of Mexican coastal cooking is its sprightly combination of plump, sweet shrimp, piquant chile, and freshly squeezed lime juice. This recipe also features fresh tomato juice, the smooth texture of avocado, and the crunch of cucumbers. The preparation here is time-consuming and a bit arcane, because no kitchen gadgets are employed, but squeezing the tomatoes by hand ensures that the "tomato red" color remains. We serve the cocktails straight up in martini glasses, each garnished with a leafy celery stalk and a wedge of lime. Bliss.*

Serves 4 to 6

FRESH SPICY TOMATO JUICE

2 pounds ripe tomatoes, cored and
    cut into 6 wedges each
2 teaspoons kosher salt
1/2 cup freshly squeezed orange juice
2 tablespoons freshly squeezed lime juice
3 teaspoons prepared horseradish
2 teaspoons Worcestershire sauce

SALSA

1/2 white onion, diced
4 chiles de arbol, stemmed and
    torn into 3 pieces each
1 tomato, cored and halved
1 1/2 teaspoons white vinegar
1/2 cup water
    Pinch of kosher salt

SHRIMP BOIL

2 quarts water
1 white onion, diced
1 red bell pepper, seeded and diced
1 carrot, peeled and diced

2 tablespoons freshly squeezed lemon juice
3 small bay leaves
1 sprig fresh thyme
2 tablespoons slightly crushed
    whole black peppercorns
1 tablespoon cayenne pepper
2 tablespoons kosher salt
1 pound (16 to 20) whole jumbo
    shrimp, unpeeled

GARNISH

1 large cucumber, peeled, seeded, and diced
2 tomatoes, seeded and diced
1 large avocado, pitted and diced
2 tablespoons cilantro leaves, coarsely chopped
4 to 6 celery stalks with leaves, for garnish
3 limes, quartered, for garnish

TO MAKE THE TOMATO JUICE, combine the tomato wedges and salt in a nonreactive bowl, gently mix, and let sit for 2 hours. Use both hands to squeeze the tomatoes into a pulp, and push them through a medium-fine metal sieve. Discard the leavings. Add the orange juice, lime juice, horseradish, and Worcestershire sauce to the tomato juice and set aside.

TO MAKE THE SALSA, place all the ingredients into a small saucepan over medium-high heat. Cook the mixture for 15 minutes, or until the volume is reduced by half. Place the mixture into the container of a blender and puree. Put all into a medium-fine sieve and strain into a bowl. Discard the leavings. Adjust the salt. Put the strained mixture into a nonreactive container, then cover and refrigerate until ready to use.

TO MAKE THE SHRIMP BOIL, place all the ingredients except the shrimp into a stockpot and bring to a boil. Add the shrimp and simmer over medium heat for 4 minutes, or until the shrimp are pink in color. Remove the pot from the burner and let the shrimp cool down in the liquid. When cooled, remove the shrimp, peel, and devein them. Cut each shrimp into 4 pieces. (Strain and freeze the shrimp boil liquid for future use in fish soups or stews.) Cover and refrigerate the shrimp. (Shrimp spoils easily, so do not keep it more than 24 hours, raw or cooked.)

TO MAKE THE GARNISH, gently combine the cucumber, tomatoes, avocado, and cilantro leaves. Divide among the serving glasses. Stir together the reserved tomato juice, shrimp, and salsa (for the faint of heart, use only half the salsa and add more to taste if needed). Pour over the vegetables and garnish with celery and lime, serving the extra lime quarters on the side.

Moroccan Eggplant with Cilantro, Ginger, and Garlic

IN THE EARLY '90S, *we were fortunate enough to work with Spanish chef Jose Ramon Lopez. He brought us this circus of pungent Mediterranean aromas and flavors. The sweetness of the eggplant marries perfectly with the sharpness of the ginger and garlic, and is rounded out by the zingy freshness of the lime juice and cilantro. I like to serve this at room temperature, letting guests mound it onto crostini for contrastive textures. Be sure to choose eggplants that are firm and shiny.*

Serves 6

EGGPLANT

3	eggplants
5	tablespoons olive oil
1	bunch cilantro, stems included
2	cloves garlic, peeled
1	tablespoon freshly grated ginger
⅛	cup water
⅛	cup freshly squeezed lime juice
½	teaspoon sea salt
1	teaspoon freshly ground black pepper

CROSTINI

1	French baguette, sliced ¼ inch thick on a slight diagonal
2 to 4	cloves garlic
½	cup extra virgin olive oil

TO ROAST THE EGGPLANT, preheat the oven to 350°F. Line a jelly-roll pan with aluminum foil. Rub each of the eggplants with 1 tablespoon of the olive oil and place them on the pan. Prick each eggplant all over with the tines of a fork, then put the pan in the oven for 50 minutes to 1¼ hours, until the eggplants collapse and are soft all over. Cooking time will vary widely due to the weight and density of individual eggplants. They should be very soft throughout when done cooking. (It's better to err on the side of overcooking rather than undercooking.) Remove the eggplants from the oven and let cool completely.

WHILE THE EGGPLANTS COOK, place the cilantro, garlic, ginger, the remaining 2 tablespoons of olive oil, water, and lime juice into the container of a blender and whirl until smooth. Add the salt and pepper and adjust for flavor balance.

WHEN THE EGGPLANTS ARE COOL, peel off the skins and discard. Cut off the stem ends and coarsely chop the eggplant. Combine with the cilantro mixture and place in a serving bowl with a serving spoon.

TO MAKE THE CROSTINI, preheat the broiler. Lay the bread slices on a baking sheet and toast under the broiler until golden brown on both sides. Remove from the broiler, and when cool enough to handle, scrape the garlic over the toasts to "grate" the garlic, giving each toast a couple of rubs of garlic on one side. Brush all with the olive oil. Place the crostini on a platter with the bowl of eggplant in the middle.

Napo's Pupusas

CHEF NAPOLEON (NAPO) LOPEZ *comes from El Salvador, where the pupusa is considered the national dish. My father declares these beauties to be the best thing he has ever eaten. Masa harina can be purchased from most supermarkets and is a staple in Latin markets. It is fire- or sun-roasted corn that is first soaked in lime water, which is made from naturally occurring calcium oxide, known as lime. The soaked wet corn is then ground into masa. When the masa is dried it is called masa harina, or masa flour. Pupusas are two discs of reconstituted masa harina that make a dough that is very pliable and fun to work with. Pupusas can be and are filled with any and every concoction. The rounds of masa are then sealed and fried on both sides and served with spicy vegetables and salsa. This recipe is the one we use at the Cafe, but let the season, your imagination, or the contents of your refrigerator determine the filling for these delectable corn discs. They can be made a day in advance and sautéed to finish.*

Serves 6

2	cups dry masa harina
11	tablespoons olive oil
2	cups water
2	zucchini, grated
$\frac{1}{2}$	large white onion, grated
1	cup fresh corn kernels (cut from about 2 ears of corn)
1	cup green chile sauce (page 66)
2	tomatoes, cored and diced into $\frac{1}{2}$-inch cubes
$1\frac{1}{2}$	teaspoons kosher salt
1	teaspoon freshly ground black pepper
$\frac{3}{4}$	cup grated Monterey Jack cheese
2	cups escabèche, for garnish (page 89)
2	cups tomato-jalapeño salsa, for garnish (page 2)
18	cilantro sprigs, for garnish

PLACE THE MASA HARINA into a bowl and add 2 tablespoons of the olive oil, mixing it with your hands.

When the ingredients are mixed enough to yield small meal, slowly add the water. Move the heel and palm of your hands in a rocking motion to blend the ingredients. (The dough will be sticky.) When all the water has been incorporated, refrigerate the dough, covering it with plastic wrap. (The dough can be made up to 24 hours in advance.)

PUT 2 TABLESPOONS of the remaining oil into a 10-inch sauté pan over medium heat. When the oil is hot, add the zucchini, onion, corn, green chile sauce, and tomatoes. Sauté the mixture for 5 minutes, then add salt and pepper to taste. Remove the mixture to a strainer and drain the juices. Press the ingredients gently with the back of a wooden spoon to remove the extra moisture.

FOR THIS STEP, you will need 6 pieces of parchment paper, cut into 16-inch by 6-inch pieces. Remove the masa from the refrigerator and form 12 balls of equal size ($1\frac{1}{2}$ ounces each). Place a piece of parchment paper on the work surface and use a brush to oil it lightly with

olive oil. (You will use about 1 tablespoon of the remaining olive oil to oil all the parchment pieces.) Place 2 of the balls near either end of the paper, then place plastic wrap over each ball. Select the bottom of a flat round plate or a container lid measuring 4 to 5 inches in diameter. Place the flat round object over each masa ball and press firmly to create a flat circle of masa. The pupusa will be very thin, about ½ inch thick. Remove the plastic and place 2 tablespoons each of the vegetable mixture and the cheese in the center of one of the masa "pancakes" and spread both over the surface of the masa. Take the unfilled masa "pancake" and fold it over onto the

first, leaving the parchment paper still attached. Press the masa cakes together and seal them by gently pressing all around the edges. Repeat to form 6 pupusas. Keep the pupusas covered until ready to sauté.

ON A HOT GRIDDLE or in a large, heated nonstick sauté pan, place 1 tablespoon of the remaining oil for each pupusa and brown each side until golden brown, about 4 minutes. To serve, pour ⅓ cup escabèche and ⅓ cup roasted tomato-jalapeño salsa onto each serving plate. Place a pupusa on top of that, and garnish each pupusa with 3 sprigs of cilantro.

Tomato Chutney

THIS IS THE PERFECT ACCOMPANIMENT *to Ghia-Pakora, which are East Indian fritters (page 95). It can also be served in place of ketchup on a great grilled hamburger, as we do at the Cafe. Asafetida, a pungent flavoring, fenugreek leaves, and black mustard seeds may all be found in Indian markets, as well as in most Asian ones.*

Makes 3 cups

1	teaspoon cumin seeds
2	teaspoons coriander seeds
1/4	tablespoon vegetable oil
1	teaspoon black mustard seeds
1/4	teaspoon asafetida
1	cup rice wine vinegar
1	cup sugar
2	cups cored, seeded, and diced ripe tomato
1	curry leaf
1	teaspoon fenugreek leaves
1/2	teaspoon turmeric
1/2	teaspoon cayenne pepper
1/4	teaspoon mace
1	tablespoon kosher salt
1/4	cup sultana golden raisins
1	tablespoon pressed garlic
1	tablespoon grated fresh ginger

TOAST THE CUMIN and coriander seeds in a dry skillet over low heat until fragrant but not browned. Put the oil into a thick-bottomed saucepan over medium heat, then add the mustard seeds and asafetida. When the seeds begin to pop, add all the other ingredients. Allow the mixture to simmer on low heat for 20 minutes, stirring occasionally. Remove, let cool, and store, covered, in the refrigerator.

RIGHT: Longtime patron David Parsons, with waiter John Roberts in the background

Dinner

Barbecoa Ruiz

TWO OF OUR STELLAR CHEFS *are brothers who grew up on their family's ranch, Rancho Villa Union, named for Pancho Villa, in Durango, Mexico. They know how to make the best barbecoa beef in the world. Here is the recipe given by Presciliano and Gabriel Ruiz for this lip-smacking Mexican dish. It's a fabulous way to feed a crowd. Barbecoa is usually cooked in a pit, so it is important to seal the cooking container with foil and keep it sealed for the duration of the cooking. You may have to search for beef cheeks, so phone your butcher to see whether they have to be specially ordered. Searching them out is worth it, because the cheeks are incredibly flavorful and "the secret" to great beef barbecoa. A leg of lamb may also be used for this recipe, but double the rest of the ingredients because the lamb will be about 5 to 6 pounds of deboned meat. (Cooking time is the same, 8 hours.) Barbecoa may be frozen for up to 2 months in small packages for future use. Serve with Chile de Arbol Salsa (see page 86). Don't forget to make a double batch of the salsa if using lamb. Have cheesecloth on hand for this recipe.*

Makes 3 cups or 12 soft tacos

2½ to 3 pounds beef cheeks, trimmed of fat
½ white onion, sliced
2 small tomatoes, cored
   and cut into small wedges
2 cloves garlic, pressed
1 jalapeño, stemmed, seeded,
   and cut into julienne
1 bay leaf
1 teaspoon dried thyme
1 teaspoon ground cumin
½ teaspoon freshly ground
   black pepper
½ teaspoon dried Mexican
   oregano or dried marjoram
1½ tablespoons white wine vinegar
2 tablespoons tequila
½ cup chicken stock
2 tablespoons freshly squeezed lime juice

¾ bottle Negro Modelo beer
2 teaspoons sea salt
12 corn tortillas, warmed
   Chile de Arbol Salsa (page 86)
4 limes, cut into wedges

PUT ALL THE INGREDIENTS except the tortillas, salsa, and limes into a tightly lidded ovenproof casserole. Cover and refrigerate for 12 hours.

REMOVE THE CASSEROLE from the refrigerator and let it come to room temperature for 1 hour, or put it in a microwave oven for 4 minutes to take the chill off.

PREHEAT THE OVEN to 400°F. Tightly wrap the entire casserole in heavy foil. Put it in the oven and let cook for 30 minutes, then turn down the temperature to 250°F. Cook for another 7 hours, then test by checking

OVERLEAF: Dinner cook Fritz Fuchs

to see whether the meat shreds easily. If it does not, cook for 1 more hour.

WHEN IT IS COOL enough to handle, shred the meat with a fork. Strain the juices through a sieve lined with a double layer of cheesecloth. Refrigerate the stock, and when solidified, discard the top layer of fat. Try to remove the jelled stock in one piece by setting the stock container into a bowl of hot water for a few seconds and then flipping the stock out upside down. Use a spoon to scrape and discard any gritty leavings that may have accumulated on the bottom of the jelly. Use this rich jellied stock immediately for another purpose, or reserve it by freezing for future use in soups or stews. Serve the barbecoa hot with warmed corn tortillas, salsa, and lime wedges.

Chard with Sultana Raisins and Sherry

CHEF JOSE RAMON LOPEZ *created this fine vegetable side dish, and it has been offered on our menu ever since. Sherry comes in a variety of styles that reflect their age and mellowing techniques. We prefer the nutty flavor of amontillado sherry. It is a perfect match for plumping the golden sultana raisins in this very Spanish take on chard. Amontillado sherry can be found at better spirits shops.*

Serves 4

- ⅓ cup organic sultana (golden) raisins
- ⅔ cup amontillado sherry
- ¼ cup pine nuts
- 1½ bunches red Swiss chard
- 2 tablespoons extra virgin olive oil
- 1 clove garlic, thinly sliced
- ¼ teaspoon kosher salt
- Pinch of freshly ground black pepper

MIX THE RAISINS and sherry in a small bowl. Let them soak for 2 hours, then drain. Toast the pine nuts in a dry skillet over medium heat, stirring frequently until slightly golden, then set aside. Remove the ribs from the Swiss chard and cut them into ½-inch slices. Coarsely chop the leaves.

IN LARGE SAUTÉ PAN warmed over medium heat, put in the olive oil, then add the garlic, and stir it for 30 seconds in the oil. Add the chard ribs and let cook for 1 minute, stirring frequently, then add the chard leaves. Cover and let it all cook down for 4 minutes, stirring occasionally. Uncover the pan, add the pine nuts and drained raisins, and cook for 1 more minute, stirring frequently. Add salt and pepper, stir once more, and serve immediately.

Cilantro Rice

THIS BRIGHT GREEN RICE *has become the mainstay of our side dishes. Cilantro is a love or hate herb by itself, but we have found that it is all love with this combination of flavors. The cilantro colors, perfumes, and adds intrigue to the rice. We serve it alongside enchiladas and all manner of Mexican-inspired dishes, as well as sautéed chicken livers (page 119).*

Serves 6

2¾   cups water

1   teaspoon kosher salt

1½   cups long-grain rice

1   cup coarsely chopped cilantro sprigs

¼   white onion, coarsely chopped

¼   cup chopped green onions, green part only

2   tablespoons freshly squeezed lime juice

½   jalapeño, stemmed and seeded

1   teaspoon olive oil

PUT THE WATER and salt into a heavy-bottomed, lidded 3-quart saucepan. Bring to a boil over high heat, then add the rice, cover, and lower the heat to very low. The rice should be ready in 20 minutes. Remove the pan from the stove, keep covered, and let it rest for 5 more minutes.

IN THE CONTAINER of a blender, put in the cilantro, white onion, green onion, lime juice, jalapeño, and olive oil. Whirl all the ingredients until incorporated, adding 1 or 2 tablespoons of water to help move the blades if necessary.

USE A FORK to stir the cilantro mixture into the rice. Serve immediately.

       RIGHT: Evening dining room manager Noreen O'Brien

Grilled Lamb Chops with Pomegranate Molasses

LAMB CHOPS ALWAYS SATISFY: *they're delicious, easy to prepare, and elegant in presentation. This quick and simple recipe was a gift from the brilliant chef Giovana, who cooked with us all too briefly. Pomegranate molasses comes in 10-ounce bottles. All you have to do is brush it on all sides of the lamb during the last 3 minutes of cooking, which lets it caramelize. The molasses tastes marvelously sour and is a perfect foil for the sweetness of the lamb. My favorite brand is Cortas, which is a product of Lebanon (see Sources, page 147).*

Serves 4

2½ to 3 pound rack of lamb with 8 chops
    (count to confirm number)
1   tablespoon fresh rosemary
    leaves, coarsely chopped
1   tablespoon minced garlic
¼   cup olive oil
1   teaspoon kosher salt
1   teaspoon freshly ground black pepper
2   tablespoons pomegranate molasses

PUT THE LAMB into a stainless steel container with the rosemary, garlic, olive oil, salt, and pepper. Marinate in the refrigerator, covered, for at least 4 hours or up to 24 hours, turning the meat once or twice. Preheat the grill or preheat an oven to 400°F.

WHEN THE GRILL IS READY, remove the lamb from the marinade and allow the oil to drip back into the container to prevent flare-ups on the grill. Place the lamb on the grill with the fleshy side down. Turn after about 7 minutes and grill the other side. If using an oven, place the meat on a rack over a foil-lined roasting pan. Cook in the oven for 20 minutes. When you have determined that the lamb is about 3 minutes away from the desired doneness, quickly brush both sides with the molasses. Turn the lamb often (with tongs, not a fork, or the juices will escape), making sure that all sides are cooked. Cook to taste, but for the most full-flavored result it is essential to leave some pink. The meat will continue to cook after leaving its heat source, so pull it off just before it reaches its desired doneness. Let the chops rest for a few minutes, covered in foil, so that the juices will be reabsorbed before cutting and serving.

Roasted Rack of Pork Loin Chops with Sage Gravy

PORK CHOPS DON'T HAVE TO BE DRY, *gray, mingy bits of flannel. For the past 40 years, big livestock business has put the American pig on a diet of steroids, hormones, antibiotics, and lean food that does not produce fat, tenderness, juiciness, or flavor. They also have kept them indoors in huge factories so that there is nothing "natural" left in the lives of these doomed creatures. At the Cafe, we use only Niman Ranch pork (and beef). Bill Niman and his staff oversee a far-flung group of Iowa family-owned pig farmers and advise them on how to raise heritage breeds, pigs that have enough fat to live a free-ranging life out of doors. Through using only organic feed, administering no drugs or hormones, and giving proper care, the pigs yield tender, juicy, and flavorful meat. Trader Joe's and other large gourmet groceries carry various cuts of both pork and beef from Niman. Niman Ranch offers a mail-order catalog (see Sources). If you can't find Niman Ranch chops, seek out other "heritage" or "heirloom" designated pork brands. The cooking instructions for the pork chops we serve are almost embarrassingly simple; there is no brining, no marinating, and no fuss. We serve them with Chard with Sultana Raisins and Sherry (page 111) and Fresh Corn Cake (page 91).*

Serves 4

PORK CHOPS

1½ teaspoons kosher salt

1 tablespoon freshly ground black pepper

2½ pounds pork chops (4 chops, ½ a rack)

SAGE GRAVY

6 tablespoons all-purpose flour

2 tablespoons cornmeal

1 teaspoon kosher salt

¼ teaspoon freshly ground black pepper

Pinch of ground white pepper

⅛ teaspoon dried basil

½ teaspoon dried sage

⅛ teaspoon dried marjoram

⅛ teaspoon dried thyme

1 tablespoon vegetable oil

3 slices thick-cut bacon, diced (freeze in advance for easy dicing)

1 cup half-and-half, heated

1 cup chicken stock, heated

1 small ripe tomato, cored and finely diced

½ teaspoon paprika

1 bunch fresh sage, for garnish

TO MAKE THE PORK CHOPS, preheat the oven to 500°F. Combine the salt and pepper and rub it all over the rack. Place the rack in a large baking pan and cook for 1¼ hours, or until the internal temperature registers 155°F on a meat thermometer inserted into the center of the chops. The meat should be ever so slightly pink. (Do not worry about parasites: 155°F will kill any possi-

bility of such.) Let the meat rest for 20 minutes, covered with foil, before cutting.

TO MAKE THE GRAVY, in a bowl, mix together the flour, cornmeal, salt, black pepper, white pepper, basil, sage, marjoram, and thyme.

PUT THE OIL INTO A SAUCEPAN over medium heat, add the bacon, and sauté until crisp. With a slotted spoon, drain and remove the bacon and set aside. Add the mixture of dry ingredients to the same saucepan

and stir with a wire balloon whisk for 2 minutes. When the mixture (roux) is bubbling, fragrant, and beginning to color, add the half-and-half and keep whisking. Just as it all comes barely to a simmer, add the chicken stock and continue to whisk until the gravy starts to thicken. Finally, whisk in the tomato and paprika. Adjust for salt.

SLICE THE CHOPS into individual servings. Ladle the gravy onto warmed serving plates and place the chop on top. Garnish with a sprig of fresh sage.

Sautéed Chicken Livers with Bacon and Marsala

FOR LOVERS OF CHICKEN LIVERS, *this is comfort food at its finest. Do not make this if you cannot find organic chicken livers. Livers are the pea trap, or clearinghouse, of any body, so all toxins, medicines, and hormones go into them and are absorbed. It is imperative to find "clean" ones. On the upside, for those of us who adore the flavor, they are rich in vitamin A and protein as well as a marvelous source of iron. Marsala is a fortified Italian wine from Sicily whose deep flavor perfectly complements these beauties. Use the secco or dry-style Marsala. This dish is sublime on top of Cilantro Rice (page 112).*

Serves 4

2	tablespoons (¼ stick) unsalted butter
2	cups sliced yellow onions
¾	teaspoon sugar
1	jalapeño, thinly sliced (optional)
12	ounces thick-cut applewood-smoked bacon strips (12 strips), cut into 1-inch pieces
1	cup all-purpose flour
1½	teaspoons kosher salt
1	teaspoon freshly ground black pepper
1	pound organic chicken livers
1	cup dry (secco) Marsala
2	cups chicken stock
½	bunch flat-leafed parsley, finely minced, for garnish

IN A LARGE SAUTÉ PAN over medium heat, melt the butter and add the onions. Stir for 1 minute, cover, and cook for 5 minutes. Lift the lid, add the sugar and jalapeño, stir, and replace the lid again for 5 more minutes. Stir the onions occasionally until golden brown and set aside.

PUT THE BACON into a large sauté pan over medium heat and sauté for 5 minutes, until it just begins to crisp.

WHILE THE BACON IS COOKING, mix together the flour, salt, and pepper in a medium bowl. Rinse the chicken livers and trim off any connective tissue. Drain them on paper towels, then roll them in the flour mixture. Add the livers to the same sauté pan and cook the livers and bacon for 10 minutes over medium heat.

ADD THE RESERVED ONIONS, Marsala, and chicken stock. Simmer over medium heat for 5 more minutes. Adjust the seasonings and serve hot over rice. Sprinkle with parsley for garnish.

Thai Green Curry

CHEF CHRISTIAN GEIDEMAN *joined our staff for two magical years and gifted us with this dynamite, complex, green curry sauce. It is served with sautéed vegetables, with the optional addition of chicken, beef, or tofu, all of it spooned over rice. Galangal is first cousin to ginger and is available either fresh or frozen. (Opt for the fresh if you have a choice.) Galangal and all the other Asian ingredients called for here are readily available from Asian markets and some natural food supermarkets.*

Serves 4

THAI GREEN CURRY SAUCE

- 2 tablespoons olive oil
- 1/2 red onion, coarsely chopped
- 1 (6-inch) stalk lemongrass, outer leaves removed, coarsely chopped
- 1 (1-inch) piece galangal, finely minced
- 2 cloves garlic, chopped
- 2 dried kaffir lime leaves
- 1 1/2 tablespoons green curry paste
- 2 tablespoons sugar
- 3 tablespoons Thai fish sauce (nam pla)
- 2 (14-ounce) cans coconut milk
- 1/2 cup chopped green onions, white and green parts
- 1/2 cup chopped cilantro, including stems and leaves, plus 4 sprigs for garnish (optional)
- 1/2 cup Thai basil, leaves only, plus 4 sprigs for garnish (optional)
- 1/2 cup loosely packed spinach leaves
- 1/2 cup water

SAUTÉED VEGETABLES

- 12 small red potatoes, cut in half
- 4 tablespoons olive oil
- 8 ounces baby carrots
- 4 small zucchini, ends trimmed and cut into 1-inch chunks
- 2 Japanese eggplants, or 1 medium eggplant, stemmed, cut into 1/2-inch rounds
- 12 shitake mushrooms, stemmed and halved
- 1 bunch beets, roasted (page 50)
- 1 pound firm organic tofu, cut into 1-inch squares (optional)
- 2 (6-ounce) filet mignon steaks, thinly sliced (optional)
- 2 boneless chicken breasts, or 4 chicken thighs, thinly sliced (optional)
- 2 cups cooked jasmine or other long-grain rice

TO MAKE THE CURRY SAUCE, place the olive oil in a large 8-quart soup pot and place over medium heat. When the oil is hot, add the onion, lemongrass, galangal, garlic, and lime leaves. Stir to combine and cook for 10 minutes. Stir in the curry paste and mix until it dissolves. Add the sugar, fish sauce, and coconut milk. Bring the sauce to a boil, then turn down the heat to low and simmer for 20 minutes, stirring occasionally. Remove from the heat and cool completely.

PLACE THE GREEN ONIONS, cilantro, Thai basil, spinach, and water into the container of a blender and puree until smooth, in batches if need be. Let cool. Stir the

puree into the cooled curry sauce, then strain through a medium-mesh sieve. Discard the solids. The sauce can be refrigerated for up to 5 days or frozen in airtight container(s) or freezer bag(s).

TO MAKE THE SAUTÉED VEGETABLES, preheat the oven to 350°F. Place the potatoes in a roasting pan, rub them with 2 tablespoons of the olive oil, and roast in the oven for 40 minutes (less if they are very small), until they are fork-tender. In a large sauté pan, heat the remaining 2 tablespoons of oil and sauté the carrots and zucchini until just fork-tender. Add the eggplant, mushrooms, cooked beets, roasted potatoes, and your choice of tofu, beef, or chicken slices. Cook until all the vegetables are fork-tender and the tofu, meat, or chicken is cooked to your liking. Mix the sauté and the curry sauce together in a large bowl. Fill 4 shallow bowls with ½ cup of the rice, and then divide the curry among them. Serve garnished with cilantro or Thai basil sprigs.

Thai Salmon in Banana Leaf with Thai Sticky Rice

THE FIRST TIME CHEF *Christian Geideman cooked this recipe in our kitchen, I knew instantly that this may be the best and single most interesting preparation for salmon I had ever encountered. It's a show-stopping presentation and sure to please your guests. Thai basil is habit-forming; it comes fresh in tied bunches and smells like a cross between basil and licorice. Galangal is cousin to fresh ginger, but is more fragrant and hotter in flavor. It can be frozen for 3 months, so it's easy to keep as a pantry item. All the other Thai ingredients can easily be kept indefinitely. Fish sauce and chile sambal come in bottles and have a very long shelf life. Both the dried shrimp and the kaffir lime leaves are also long-lived. All these delectable ingredients can be found in any Asian market and in most natural food stores. They are the usual suspects in most Thai dishes—so once on the road to Thai cuisine, you will be using all of these again and again. The investment is so small for such a great reward, so do add these to your pantry and try them in soups and other dishes where fragrance, spice, and complexity are desired. At the Cafe, we serve this with Thai long-grain sticky rice.*

Serves 6

3 cups Thai long-grain sticky rice

2 cups fresh Thai basil leaves

2 cloves garlic

1 (2-inch) piece galangal, finely minced

¼ tablespoon sugar

¼ tablespoon fish sauce (nam pla)

2 tablespoons chile sambal

½ teaspoon shrimp paste, or

    1 teaspoon ground dried shrimp

2 dried kaffir lime leaves

¼ cup finely minced lemongrass, white part only

¼ cup water

6 (6-ounce) fresh wild salmon filets, uniform in size, all bones removed

6 banana leaves, thawed, cut into 11-inch by 11-inch squares

6 banana-leaf strips, cut ½ inch wide and 10 inches long (tie 2 together if necessary)

RINSE THE RICE in a fine-mesh metal sieve until the water runs clear. Soak the rice, covered in water, for at least 3 hours and up to 8 hours. Line a large metal sieve with cheesecloth, then place the soaked rice in it. Place the sieve over a pot of boiling water, being careful not to let the water touch the rice. Cover the pot tightly with aluminum foil. Cook for 25 minutes, or until the rice is opalescent in appearance. Be sure to check the water for possible replenishment during the cooking time because it may boil away.

PREPARE A GRILL or preheat the oven to 375°F. Place the Thai basil, garlic, minced galangal, sugar, fish sauce, chile sambal, shrimp paste, kaffir lime leaves, minced lemongrass, and water into the bowl of a food processor fitted with a steel blade, or into the container of a blender. Process until the ingredients have become a paste. (Add a bit more water if needed to move the blades of the blender.)

TO ASSEMBLE THE SALMON PACKETS, place a filet of salmon diagonally at one corner of the banana leaf. Place 2 tablespoons of the blended mixture on top and spread to cover the salmon. Roll the salmon filet toward the opposite corner. At the midway point, fold in the other two adjacent corners over the salmon, then continue to roll the filet to the opposite corner. Tie the package with the banana-leaf strip. Repeat until all are rolled and tied, then lay them out on a baking sheet or put directly on the grill, at least 3 inches from the flame. Bake for 15 minutes or grill for 6 minutes per side. Serve in their packages and let your diners open them. Do not take the salmon out of the leaf, but rather use the leaf as a doily. Serve with the sticky rice.

Sugar Pumpkins Filled with Vegetable Stew in Chipotle Cream Sauce

WHEN FALL BEGINS, *all of us eagerly await the pumpkin harvest so that we can make and enjoy serving these delight-filled pumpkins. Sugar pumpkins are the uniformly 1-pound pumpkins that can easily be found in natural groceries or better supermarkets. Since this is a harvest dish, feel free to select any combination of vegetables you may need to use up from the garden or from harvesting the refrigerator. The little pumpkins are cooked until the flesh is soft enough to be eaten along with the filling, so do provide a soup spoon and encourage your diners to dig in. We serve the personal pumpkins in shallow pasta bowls with a large purple kale leaf acting as a doily so that the pumpkin will not slip about the plate.*

Serves 4

4 (1-pound) sugar pumpkins

6 tablespoons (¾ stick) unsalted butter

1 white onion, diced

4 cloves garlic, minced

2 carrots, peeled and diced

2 stalks celery, diced

1⅓ pounds fresh cultivated button mushrooms, sliced

2 cups portobello mushrooms, stems and gills removed, diced into ½-inch cubes

2 teaspoons fresh thyme leaves

1 tablespoon chipotle puree

1 chipotle chile en adobo

1½ cups heavy cream

¾ cup vegetable stock (store-bought organic is fine)

1 tablespoon dry (secco) Marsala

1 teaspoon kosher salt

1 teaspoon freshly ground pepper

⅛ teaspoon freshly ground nutmeg

¼ cup olive oil

1 cup fresh corn kernels (cut from about 2 ears of corn)

2 cups diced zucchini

8 sprigs parsley, finely minced, for garnish

4 large purple kale leaves, for garnish

8 pieces crostini (page 101)

PREHEAT THE OVEN to 350°F. Cut the pumpkin stems down so that they are just 1 inch high, then cut the lids off the pumpkins, as you would for making a jack-o'-lantern. Scoop out the seeds and scrape out any seeds attached to the top. (Discard or reserve the seeds for other uses.) Place the pumpkins in a large roasting pan and fill each one two-thirds full with hot water. Replace the pumpkin lids. Add enough hot water to the pan to have 1 inch of water around the pumpkins. Cover the pan completely and tightly with foil and bake for 60 minutes, or until the pumpkin flesh is fork-tender on the inside but the shell still holds its shape. Remove the pumpkins from the pan and carefully drain the water. Keep warm.

HEAT 4 TABLESPOONS of the butter in a large saucepan over medium heat and add the onion, garlic, carrot,

and celery. Sauté until the onions start to become translucent. Add both types of mushrooms and thyme and cook the mixture for 15 minutes longer. Stir frequently. (The mushrooms will cook down and lose their moisture.) Set aside.

COMBINE THE CHIPOTLE PUREE, chipotle chile, and cream in the container of a blender. Put the mixture into a saucepan, then add the stock and Marsala. Bring the mixture to a boil, then reduce the heat and allow it to simmer for 10 minutes, stirring frequently, until the mixture thickens slightly. Season the sauce with salt, pepper, and nutmeg and set aside.

IN A LARGE SAUTÉ PAN, heat the olive oil and remaining 2 tablespoons of butter until hot. Add the corn and zucchini. Sauté over medium-high heat until the corn starts to brown, about 7 minutes, stirring frequently. Stir in the vegetable mixture. Season with additional salt and pepper if needed, and fill each pumpkin with one-quarter of the vegetable mixture. Gently reheat the chipotle sauce and ladle over the vegetables in the pumpkin. Sprinkle with the parsley. Replace the lid, place the pumpkins in pasta bowls on top of the kale leaves, and serve immediately with warm crostini on the side.

ABOVE: Dinner chef, Presciliano Ruiz

Dessert

Mocha Pot de Crème

THIS SILKEN MOCHA PUDDING RECIPE *comes from pastry chef Stephanie Morris, who practiced her art of dessert making at the Cafe for many years. This is decidedly an adult chocolate dessert, but it will make a child out of you and your guests when you clamor for more. Be sure to use decaffeinated coffee, because the chocolate will be stimulant enough.*

Serves 6

1½	cups whole milk
1½	cups heavy cream
½	cup sugar
¼	cup finely ground decaffeinated espresso beans
¼	cup crushed decaffeinated espresso beans
8	ounces bittersweet chocolate, coarsely chopped
8	organic egg yolks
6	espresso beans, for garnish

REFRIGERATE 6 EMPTY 4-OUNCE RAMEKINS. Place the milk, cream, sugar, and both measures of espresso beans into a saucepan over medium heat. Simmer and stir to dissolve the sugar. Turn the heat down to low and allow the mixture to steep for 30 minutes. Use a fine-mesh strainer to strain the cream mixture into a bowl. Rinse the saucepan out well and dry it before reuse. Pour the cream back into the saucepan, return it to the stove, and add the chocolate. Allow the chocolate to melt over low heat, stirring occasionally.

WHILE THE CHOCOLATE IS MELTING, whisk the egg yolks in a bowl until well mixed. Temper the yolks by whisking in ¼ cup of the cream and chocolate mixture, then pour the yolk mixture back into the remainder of the cream. Stir over low heat until the mixture coats the back of a wooden spoon. Pour into the chilled ramekins and refrigerate until set, about 3 hours. Serve chilled, and garnish the top of each serving with a single espresso bean, placed split side up.

David's Perfect Pumpkin Pie

DAVID COULSON, *our general manager, has a passion for pumpkin pie. He has developed this pie recipe over two decades, and for his taste this is THE recipe. Whole-wheat pastry flour may be purchased in any natural food grocery or almost any supermarket. Note that this recipe is for two pies, because I'm guessing that there is usually a crowd when pumpkin pies are involved. To scrape the vanilla bean, split the bean and scrape out the insides with a sharp knife.*

Makes two 9-inch pies

WHOLE-WHEAT PIE CRUST

2½	cups whole-wheat pastry flour
2	pinches of sea salt
¼	teaspoon freshly ground nutmeg
1	cup (2 sticks) unsalted butter, well chilled
¼	cup ice-cold water
1	large organic egg beaten with 2 tablespoons water

FILLING

8	large organic eggs
1¾	cups maple syrup
1	cup sour cream
4	cups pumpkin puree (two 15-ounce cans)
½	cup dark unsulphured molasses
2	tablespoons ground ginger
½	teaspoon ground cloves
½	teaspoon freshly ground nutmeg
½	teaspoon ground allspice
¼	teaspoon cayenne pepper
2	pinches of sea salt
1½	teaspoons vanilla extract
8	ounces evaporated milk or heavy cream

CHANTILLY CREAM

1	cup heavy cream
	Scrapings of ½ whole vanilla bean
3	tablespoons powdered sugar

TO MAKE THE PIE CRUSTS, put the flour into a large mixing bowl and mix in the salt and nutmeg. Add the butter and incorporate, either by using a pastry cutter or your hands, "washing" the ingredients between both hands until the mixture resembles coarse cornmeal. (The latter method is recommended.) Add the ice water and toss lightly with a fork. Press the mixture together, being careful to knead it as little as possible. (Working the dough too much will lead to a tough crust.) If the dough is not sticking together, add another 1 or 2 tablespoons of water. (Too much additional water will steam the crust and also make it tough.) Form the dough quickly into 2 equal-sized balls and wrap tightly in plastic wrap. Chill in the refrigerator for about 1 hour to let the gluten in the dough rest. (If you skip this step, the crust will most likely be tough in texture.) While the dough is chilling, make the pie filling.

TO MAKE THE FILLING, crack the eggs into a large mixing bowl and beat them with a wire whisk. Add the maple

syrup and whisk again. Blend in the sour cream, then add the remainder of the ingredients and mix well. Set aside.

PREHEAT THE OVEN to 350°F. To roll out the dough, sprinkle some flour onto a large board or cool counter-top and pat the dough into a circle. Use a well-floured rolling pin to roll the dough away from yourself, beginning in the middle of the dough. With each pass of the pin, pick up the dough with your hands and turn it one-quarter turn. When the dough has become slightly larger than the circumference of the pie pan, roll half of the crust up and around the pin. Carefully drag the dough to the pan and fit the dough over half the pan and unwind the pin to lay out the rest. Gently fit the dough into the bottom of the pan and crimp all around the edge with your fingers, or press the tines from the back of a fork all around the edge.

REPEAT THE PROCESS for the second pie. Brush the egg and water mixture thoroughly all over both crusts to seal them and make them impervious to the wet filling. Bake the crusts for 12 minutes. Completely cool the crusts before filling, placing the pans either on a cooling rack, over two large crossed serving spoons, or over any tool that will elevate the pans. This way air will circulate all around the pies and prevent moisture from condensing on the bottoms of the crusts as they cool. Turn up the oven to 400°F.

POUR THE PUMPKIN MIXTURE into the 2 now cooled prebaked pie crusts and bake at 400°F for 15 minutes. Reduce the temperature to 350°F and bake for an additional 45 minutes, or until the pies are golden on top. Test the pies by inserting a knife blade into the center of the pies. If the blade comes out clean, the pies are done. Let cool.

TO MAKE THE CREAM, use an electric mixer fitted with a wire whisk attachment. Put the heavy cream and the vanilla bean scrapings into the mixer's metal bowl. (Reserve the remaining ½ of the vanilla bean. You can store the bean by burying it in powdered sugar to flavor the sugar for future use.) Whip the cream until almost stiff, add the powdered sugar, and continue whipping until the cream holds peaks.

SERVE THE PIE AT ROOM TEMPERATURE or store, covered, in the refrigerator. Place a dollop of the cream on top of each pie or serve it alongside with a spoon for your guests to help themselves.

Flan de Coco

THIS QUINTESSENTIAL MEXICAN DESSERT *comes from Iliana de la Vega, chef/owner of El Naranjo Restaurant in Oaxaca City, Mexico. It has a smooth and delicate texture under its rich, red-brown syrup. Use canned cream of coconut that is used for making piña coladas, found in most supermarkets. We have added coconut essence that can be found in little bottles in the spice section of most groceries. Ramekins are individual, straight-sided ceramic baking and serving dishes that come in 4-ounce and 6-ounce sizes. You can readily buy these at kitchen departments of large houseware stores or from kitchen specialty shops.*

Serves 6

¾ cup sugar
   Juice of ½ lemon
¼ cup water
½ cup cream of coconut (Coco López brand)
½ cup sweetened condensed milk
1¾ cups whole milk
¾ cup shredded sweetened coconut
6 large organic eggs
2 teaspoons coconut essence

PREHEAT THE OVEN to 300°F. Place the sugar, lemon juice, and water into a heavy-bottomed saucepan over low heat. Cook until the sugar mixture is melted, caramelized, and quite dark in color. Divide the mixture equally among 6 (6-ounce) ramekins.

PLACE THE CREAM OF COCONUT, sweetened condensed milk, whole milk, shredded sweetened coconut, eggs, and coconut essence into the container of a blender, process, and distribute evenly among the ramekins. Cover each with a square of aluminum foil. Place the ramekins into a deep-sided pan large enough to accommodate them. Fill the pan with water to reach halfway up the sides of each ramekin. Bake for 1 hour. Let cool completely and refrigerate until ready to serve.

TO SERVE THE FLAN, run a knife all around the edge to loosen the flan from the ramekin's edge. Hold an individual plate over the top of the ramekin, then turn and quickly flip both together in one quick motion to release the flan and its syrup onto the plate. Carefully lift the ramekin and let any residual syrup flow over the top of the flan.

Meyer Lemon Ice Cream with Honeycomb Drizzle

ONE MEMORABLE EVENING, *while dining at my beloved Manka's Inverness Lodge in Inverness, California, Margaret Grade, chef and proprietress, sent out a fabulous Meyer lemon ice cream with a hunk of honeycomb perched atop the scoops. Honey was slowly oozing down the lemon ice cream and I was knocked out by the flavors and presentation, so this is our homage to Margaret and Manka's, with gratitude for yet another stellar experience. Meyer lemons are available from November through May. Originally from China, these little round lemons are sweeter than regular lemons, and are thought to have been perhaps married to an orange when first cultivated. They have a lower acid content than their first cousins, those pointy-end thick-skinned relations. Meyers may be difficult to find, but they are worth the hunt. (Ask your favorite produce manager to order some.) They may be kept in the vegetable crisper in the refrigerator for up to 2 weeks.*

Makes 1 quart

 3   cups heavy cream
 1   cup whole milk
 1   cup plus 2 tablespoons sugar
     3 tablespoons lemon zest (from about
       6 Meyer lemons)
     Juice of 12 Meyer lemons
10   large organic egg yolks
 1   teaspoon lemon extract
 8   ounces honeycomb

PLACE THE CREAM, milk, sugar, lemon zest, and lemon juice into a heavy-bottomed saucepan and stir to combine. Bring the mixture to a boil over high heat, immediately reduce the heat to low, and simmer for 30 minutes, stirring occasionally.

MEANWHILE, whisk the egg yolks in a bowl until they are lemon-yellow in color. To ensure that the eggs do not curdle, whisk in ½ cup of the hot cream mixture in two ¼-cup measures, whisking between additions. Add all of the yolks back into the cream and cook over medium heat, stirring constantly, until the mixture thickens and coats the back of a spoon. Remove the mixture from the heat and stir in the lemon extract.

CHILL THE ICE CREAM mixture until very cold, either overnight in the refrigerator or in an ice bath.

FREEZE THE MIXTURE according to your ice cream machine's manufacturer's instructions. To serve, top scoops of the ice cream with a generous piece of the honeycomb and let the honey drip down the ice cream.

PASQUAL'S™

St. Andre and Goat Gouda Cheeses with Rye
and Oat Bran Flatbreads and Membrillo
11.

Garnets in Blood

Peach Almond Strudel with Chantilly Cream

Maple Baked Pumpkin

Tiramisu Cake

Apple Raisin Crisp

Malted Coffee Ice Cream with Fudge Sauce

Lychee Sorbet

An Assortment of Our Cookies with Chocolate Hazelnut Bark
8.
Chef's Sampler for Two
14.

Royal Tokaji Red Label 1996 Glass 8.	Domaine de Durban Beaumes de Venise 2000 Glass 7.
Gould Campbell 10 Year Tawny Glass 8.	Gutierrez Casta Diva Cosecha Miel 1999 Glass 6.
Emilio Lustau Dry Oloroso "Don Nuno" Sherry Glass 6.	Gould Campbell 1996 LBV Glass 5.

Clos Lapeyre Jurançon 2001
Half Bottle 34. Glass 7.

Press Pot Organic Coffee /12 oz 4.75
Espresso 2.25, Double Espresso 3.25, Cappuccino, Latte 3.95,
Mocha Latte, White Chocolate Mocha Latte 4.25,
Mexican Hot Chocolate 3.95,
Chai (regular or decaf) with Steamed Milk 3.95
(Soy Milk Available 4.25)
Hot Teas with Caffeine – British Breakfast, Earl Grey, Prince of Wales, Green Tea
with Toasted Rice, Blackberry Sage, Ginger Peach
Herbal Teas – Chamomile Lemon, Orange Ginger Mint, Cardamon Cinnamon and
Ginseng–Peppermint, Mango Ceylon 1.50

Pastry Chefs–Gabriel Ruiz and Elizabeth Quirante

121 DON GASPAR SANTA FE NEW MEXICO 87501 (505) 983-9340 FAX 988 4645

Prickly Pear Cactus Sorbet

THIS IS A FLAT-OUT FUN DESSERT *developed by chef Gabriel Ruiz. The brilliant magenta color is derived from the fruit of the prickly pear cactus and is unforgettable in both appearance and flavor. Don't worry: there are no spines on the cactus fruit, so no special defensive equipment is necessary. This is a perfect ending to any south-of-the-border fiesta.*

Makes 1 quart

1¾ pounds prickly pear cactus
      fruit (about 18 fruit)
½ cup sugar
½ cup water
1 tablespoon freshly squeezed lime juice

WASH, PEEL, AND QUARTER the prickly pears. Puree them in the bowl of a food processor fitted with a steel blade or in the container of a blender. (If needed, add a tablespoon of water to move the blender's blades.) Strain the puree through a sieve into a bowl and set the resulting puree aside. Discard the strained pulp.

PLACE THE SUGAR and water into a saucepan and bring to a boil. Stir until the sugar is dissolved and remove from the heat. Let cool completely.

ADD THE SUGAR SYRUP and lime juice to the puree and stir to combine. Chill in the refrigerator until very cold. Freeze in an ice cream machine according to the manufacturer's instructions. Cover the finished sorbet and freeze until firm.

Melon and Chardonnay Granita

THIS SIMPLE AND EASY *concoction will please you and your guests with its concentrated flavor and lightness. Melons always remind me of captured sunshine, with their exquisite color, vibrancy, and embodied flavor of a growing season's culmination.*

Makes 2 quarts

2   cups sugar

2   cups water

3   pounds ripe cantaloupe, casaba, or Crenshaw
      melon, peeled, seeded, and coarsely chopped

¾   cup Chardonnay wine

HEAT THE SUGAR AND WATER in a saucepan until the sugar is dissolved. Chill the syrup thoroughly. Puree the melon of choice along with the syrup in the container of a food processor fitted with a metal blade, or in the container of a blender. Add the Chardonnay and stir to incorporate. Pour the mixture into a shallow dish of 4-quart capacity, and place in the freezer. Scrape through the entire mixture with a fork, hourly, to achieve a granular texture until it is completely frozen, about 6 hours.

Nectarine Raspberry Crisp

I GET DITZY ABOUT NECTARINES, *indeed, all stone fruits: peaches, apricots, and all the varieties of plums. Raspberries, blackberries, huckleberries, and blueberries also make me slaphappy. Please regard this recipe as a template for your favorite combinations of fruit in high summer. I like to make zest with a microplane rasp. It is easily found in any kitchen supply shop, and it will change your cooking habits. It's so much fun to use such an efficient tool that you will look for excuses to add zest to everything! My preference is not to sully the exquisite fresh fruit in this dish with white gooey toppings, but there are those who swear the experience would be incomplete without it, so you may have to acquire vanilla ice cream, half-and-half, or whipping cream for topping. This recipe was developed by pastry chef Elizabeth Quirante.*

Serves 8 to 12

1	cup plus 2 tablespoons (2¼ sticks) unsalted butter
14	fresh nectarines, peeled, halved, pitted, and sliced
2	cups fresh raspberries
1	cup granulated sugar
½	cup freshly squeezed lemon juice
4	teaspoons grated lime zest
½	cup firmly packed brown sugar
1½	cups all-purpose flour
3	cups Linda's Golden Granola (page 11)
1½	teaspoons cinnamon
1½	teaspoons nutmeg
½	teaspoon kosher salt

PREHEAT THE OVEN to 350°F. Use a paper towel to rub 2 tablespoons of the butter over the inside of a 9-inch by 13-inch glass baking dish.

PLACE THE NECTARINES into the baking dish and scatter the raspberries over them. Sprinkle the granulated sugar over the fruit, drizzle the lemon juice over the fruit, and sprinkle the lime zest over all.

IN A LARGE MIXING BOWL, stir together the brown sugar, flour, granola, cinnamon, nutmeg, and salt. Cut the remaining 1 cup of butter into ¼-inch-thick slices. Use a pastry cutter or your hands to rub the butter into the mixture until it resembles a coarse meal.

SPREAD THE TOPPING evenly over the fruit and bake for 1 hour, until the topping is golden brown and the fruit is tender. Serve warm.

Shortbread Cookies

PASTRY CHEF STEPHANIE MORRIS *gets the credit for this supremely tasty cookie. They are sturdy enough to ice, decorate, and, if need be, transport to a celebration site. Cookie cutters are widely available in a profusion of shapes that go far beyond the usual, so have fun collecting some eccentric ones.*

Makes 24 cookies

COOKIES

2   **cups (4 sticks) unsalted butter**
1   **cup granulated sugar**
4   **cups all-purpose flour**
⅓   **teaspoon sea salt**
2   **tablespoons firmly packed lemon or orange zest**
2   **tablespoons candied ginger (optional)**
2   **tablespoons poppy seeds (optional)**

ICING

1   **cup powdered sugar**
2   **tablespoons freshly squeezed lemon juice**
    Scant ¼ cup water
    Food coloring
    Decorative cookie sprinkles (optional)

TO MAKE THE COOKIES, put the butter and granulated sugar into the bowl of an electric mixer fitted with a paddle attachment. Cream the butter and sugar until incorporated. When completely mixed, scrape down the sides of the bowl and add the flour, salt, and desired flavoring options. Turn on the mixer and slowly mix until just combined. (Do not overmix or the cookies will be hard and tough.) Divide the dough in half and make 2 balls. Cover each ball with plastic wrap and refrigerate for at least 2 hours and up to 24 hours.

PREHEAT THE OVEN TO 300° and grease 2 cookie sheets with butter or vegetable spray. Place the dough on a well-floured surface and use a floured rolling pin to roll out the dough to a ¼-inch thickness. Use cookie cutter(s) to cut out the desired shapes. Place the cookies on the greased cookie sheets and bake for 20 minutes, or until lightly brown. Gather up any scraps from the cutting process, roll again, and proceed as before. Cool the cookies on cooling racks. When completely cool, ice each cookie.

TO MAKE THE ICING, combine the powdered sugar, lemon juice, and water in a mixing bowl, stir, and divide into as many bowls as you want colors for your icing. Add 1 or 2 drops of food coloring to each bowl. Use a bag fitted with the desired tips for decorative designs. If you do not have a pastry bag, try this trick: fill plastic sandwich-sized bags with icing. Use a pair of sharp scissors to snip off a tiny corner of the bag, creating a small hole out of which the icing can be squeezed for writing or decoration. Sprinkles must be added immediately, before the icing dries.

Tahitian Chocolate Lace Cookies

I THOUGHT IT WOULD BE FUN *to "tropicalize" the classic Italian Florentine cookie recipe. My version includes macadamia nuts instead of the usual hazelnuts, and dried mango, papaya, and coconut instead of the ubiquitous candied citron and cherries. We use 70 percent Valrhona chocolate, easily obtainable in large supermarkets. I highly recommend the purchase of a Silpat or two. This is a food-safe high-heat plastic sheet that lines the cookie sheet and makes cookie removal a snap. Silpats are always stocked in good kitchen shops. While you are purchasing the Silpat also consider buying another new-to-market wonder, a silicone brush: the chocolate will be easy to brush onto the cookie and there is no clumping on the brush or shedding of bristles along the way. A candy thermometer is also a must in a well-stocked kitchen. By all means, obtain one so that you can temper the chocolate.*

Makes 36 cookies

- 1 cup macadamia nuts
- ¼ cup shredded sweetened coconut
- 2 ounces dried mango
- 2 ounces dried papaya
- ¼ cup all-purpose flour
- ⅔ cup heavy cream
- ⅔ cup sugar
- ¼ teaspoon sea salt
- 4 ounces semisweet or bittersweet chocolate

PREHEAT THE OVEN to 300°F. Mix the macadamia nuts and coconut in a shallow roasting pan and bake for about 10 minutes, stirring frequently, until golden brown. Let cool.

IN THE BOWL OF A FOOD PROCESSOR fitted with a steel blade, put in the nuts, coconut, dried fruit, and flour. Pulse 3 times until the mixture is chopped but still coarse. Set aside.

PUT THE CREAM, sugar, and salt into a small saucepan and cook over medium heat, stirring, until the sugar dis-solves. Let cool. Add the chopped mixture to the sweetened cream and stir until incorporated. Chill thoroughly in the refrigerator.

PREHEAT THE OVEN to 350°F. When the mixture is very cold, measure 1 tablespoon of the dough, form it into a ball, and place it on a nonstick cookie sheet. Repeat, spacing the dough balls 2 inches apart, because the cookies will spread as they bake. (The baking sheet will hold about 8 cookies.) Bake the cookies for 15 minutes, then cool them on a cooling rack. Repeat until all the cookies have been baked.

WHEN THE COOKIES HAVE COOLED, melt 3 ounces of the chocolate in a saucepan over low heat, stirring, until it is melted. Remove from the heat and add in the remaining 1 ounce of chocolate until the temperature reaches 90°F on a candy thermometer. Work quickly to brush the chocolate over the bottom of each cookie with a silicone brush. Return each brushed cookie to the cooling rack and let the chocolate harden, chocolate side up. Serve the cookies chocolate side down.

Sources

Café Pasqual's
121 Don Gaspar
Santa Fe, NM 87501
800-722-7672
505-983-9340
fax: 505-988-4645
www.pasquals.com
info@pasquals.com

Restaurant, retail store, and Internet catalog
Red chile dried sauce mix with recipe; includes
  ancho, guajillo, and chile de arbol
Green chile dried sauce mix with recipe
Berbere spice
Five-Grain Cereal
Linda's Golden Granola

Adriana's Caravan
78 Grand Central Terminal
New York, NY 10017
800-316-0820
www.adrianascaravan.com

Retail store and mail-order catalog
Pomegranate molasses
Dried chiles, powdered chiles, canned chiles
Berbere spice

Chile Today—Hot Tamale
31 Richboynton Road
Dover, NJ 07801
800-468-7377
www.chiletoday.com

Mail-order catalog
Dried chiles, powdered chiles

The CMC Company
P. O. Drawer 322
Avalon, NJ 08202
800-262-2780
www.thecmccompany.com
sales@thecmccompany.com

Mail-order catalog
Pomegranate molasses
Mexican ingredients
Dried chiles, powdered chiles, canned chiles
Asafetida and Indian ingredients
Thai ingredients

Erawan Thai Market
1463 University Avenue
Berkeley, CA 94702
510-849-9707

Retail store and mail-order catalog
Thai ingredients

Frieda's
4465 Corporate Center Drive
Los Alamitos, CA 90720
800-421-9477
www.friedas.com

Mail-order catalog
Fresh and dried chiles

GroceryThai.com
13138 Meyer Road
Whittier, CA 90605
818-469-9407
www.grocerythai.com
info@grocerythai.com

Mail-order catalog
Thai ingredients

Herbs of Mexico
3903 Whittier Boulevard
Los Angeles, CA 90023
323-261-2521
www.herbsofmexico.com

Mail-order catalog
Mexican and other worldly herbs

Heritage Foods USA
2370 East Stadium Boulevard, Suite 007
Ann Arbor, MI 48104
212-980-6603
www.heritagefoodsusa.com

Mail-order catalog
Iroquois roasted white corn flour

ImportFood.com
P. O. Box 2054
Issaquah, WA 98027
888-618-8424
www.importfood.com
info@importfood.com

Mail-order catalog
Fresh Thai produce and ingredients

Kitchen/Market
218 Eighth Avenue
New York, NY 10011
888-468-4433
www.kitchenmarket.com

Retail store and mail-order catalog
Chiles
Thai ingredients
Herbs and spices

MexGrocer.com
7445 Girard Avenue, Suite 6
La Jolla, CA 92037
877-463-9476
www.mexgrocer.com

Mail-order catalog
Mexican chiles, spices, herbs, and specialty ingredients

Niman Ranch
1025 East 12th Street
Oakland, CA 94606
866-808-0340
www.nimanranch.com

Mail-order catalog
Naturally raised beef and pork

Pendery's
304 E. Belknap Street
Fort Worth, TX 76102
800-533-1870
www.penderys.com

Mail-order catalog
Chiles and spices

Penzeys Spices
19300 West Janacek Court
Brookfield, WI 53008
800-741-7787
www.penzeys.com

Retail stores and mail-order catalog
Spices, herbs, and seasonings

Pinewood Community Farms
13466 4 Mile Level Road
Gowanda, NY 14070
716-532-5241

Mail-order catalog
Iroquois roasted white corn flour

Temple of Thai
P. O. Box 112
Carroll, LA 51401
877-811-8773
www.templeofthai.com
customerservice@templeofthai.com

Mail-order catalog
Thai ingredients

Thai Grocery
5014 N. Broadway Street
Chicago, IL 60640
773-561-5345

Mail-order catalog
Thai ingredients

Thai Herbs & Spices
P. O. Box 151835
Austin, TX 78715-1835
512-507-0981
www.thaiherbs.com
admin@thaiherbs.com

Mail-order catalog
Thai ingredients

Tierra Vegetables
220 Pleasant Avenue
Santa Rosa, CA 95403
1-888-7TIERRA
www.tierravegetables.com

Mail-order catalog
Garden fresh vegetables and chiles

Index